ADJUSTING

EXPECTATIONS

BY ROY & LAINEY HITCHMAN

ADJUSTING

EXPECTATIONS

Copyright © 2016 by Roy & Lainey Hitchman

Cover by: Lainey Hitchman

Editor: Roy Hitchman

ISBN: 9781911176046
Book Website
www.hitchedtogether.com
Email: info@hitchedtogether.com

Give feedback on the book at:
feedback@hitchedtogether.com

EXPEC✝ATIONS

ADJUSTING

BY Roy & Lainey Hitchman

Book 2
✝ Cultural Marriage Series

OTHER BOOKS IN THIS SERIES

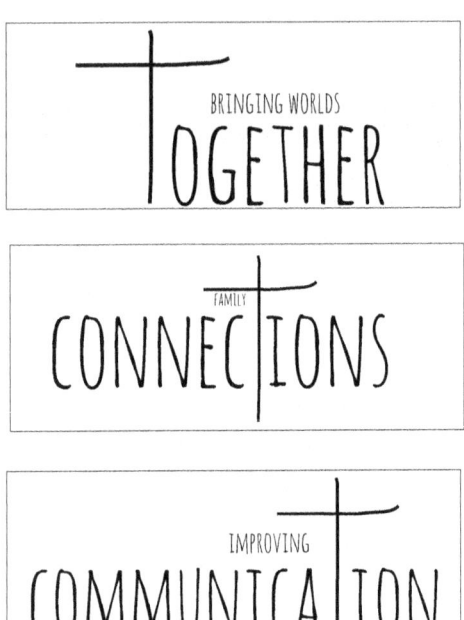

Acknowledgments

How can we say a big enough thank you to our friends and family. Your help and support far exceeded our expectations! When we needed encouragement you were there, when we needed advice during this project you gave it! We are thankful that you helped us set realistic goals, manage our expectations and do some adjusting!

Preface

A light turned on during the process of writing 'Bringing Worlds Together' the first of the Cross-cultural Marriage Series. It seems every marriage is stamped with an exclusive blend of cultures; they are also influenced by unique expectations.

Having unmet expectations has an adverse effect on relationships. In marriages where expectations have been too high, disappointment and blame often go hand in hand. People can feel let down or wronged. It doesn't need to be this way. It's possible to remove those rose coloured glasses and have a more realistic idea of what to expect in marriage.

This book should help you to recognise what your expectations are, how they were formed and if any need adjustment. You'll have an opportunity to manage your expectations and set realistic ones. You'll also have the opportunity to assess whether, like us, you have a tendency to be a little too hard on yourself.

Adjusting Expectations hasn't been written by people who pretend to have it all together. Roy and I have set expectations too high, set them too low and struggled to be realistic. We hope our experience will help you on your journey through married life.

CONTENTS

Adjusting expec ations   3

     Acknowledgments   5

     Preface   6

What did you expect?   10

     What is an Expectation?   13

     Everyone Expects Something   15

     Inaccurate measurements   22

The Formation of Expectations   26

     The Early Years   27

     Pre-Teen Years   32

     Teens and Early Twenties   33

     Promises, Promises!   36

Changing Expectations   41

     Managing Your Expectations   46

     What can Change?   49

     Changing Attitudes   56

Changing Habits	59
Expectations of Love & Romance	63
Adam's Expectations	64
Expectations of Love	68
Did you expect it to be easy?	68
Expecting a soulmate	70
The Danger of Believing in Soul mates	72
Did you expect it to last forever?	75
Eternal Promise	77
Expectations of Romance	79
Romantic Heroes	80
Unromantic Heroes	82
Expectations of Intimacy	85
Half-Hearted & Hard Hearted	88
Snake-Oil	90
False Expectations	91
Who told you that?	94
What does God Know about Sex	96
God's Design for Intimacy	98

What does God Expect?	106
God Expects Us to Walk In Love	107
God Expects You to Grow Together	111
God Expects You to Study	113
God Expects You to Apply	115
God Expects us to Have Faith	119
When Expectations Go Very Wrong	120
Emotional Abuse	123
Spiritual Abuse	125
Physical Abuse	127
Why Abuse Happens	130
Selfishness	130
Blame	131
Fundamental Attribution Error	132
Fear	134
What to Do if Abuse Happens	135
Releasing from Expectations	139
Expect to Blessed	140
Bibliography	143
Biography	146

WHAT DID YOU EXPECT?

What did you expect?

It is universally considered that Albert Einstein was a smart man. If the attribution of this quote is correct it confirms his intelligence!

> "Women marry men hoping they will change. Men marry women hoping they won't change. Inevitably both will be disappointed".
> Albert Einstein.

Roy:

I remember when Lainey and I married, almost three decades ago! We were both so excited about the life we were going to live together and couldn't wait to tie the knot and move in together. We had so many expectations of what married life was going to be like! For me it was expectations of not needing to wash and iron, expectations of fantastic food (no cooking required and definitely no washing up because I now had a loving wife), and, of course, expectations of fantastic sex every day!

It didn't take us long to realise that our expectations were unrealistic! It didn't take much longer for a little disappointment to set in. We started to understand that married life was going to take more work than we had expected and give fewer benefits than we had hoped for. I am confident that most of you could tell a similar story. Many of you probably felt a degree of disappointment, and some of you still do.

As you read this book, you will have an opportunity to take a look at your marriages, address the unrealistic expectations, and deal with the disappointments. In a way, it is an opportunity to make a fresh start and build your marriage on something more solid than the sand of hopes and dreams. It's your chance to strengthen your foundations by building on realistic expectations that come from God's guidance for your lives together.

PHILIPPIANS 1:6 (ESV)
AND I AM SURE OF THIS,
THAT HE WHO BEGAN A GOOD WORK IN YOU
WILL BRING IT TO COMPLETION AT THE DAY OF JESUS CHRIST.

What is an Expectation?

So let's take a step back and make sure we all understand what an expectation is. It's important to know what it is and what it is not.

Expectation:

- "An expectation is a strong belief that something will happen, or be the case in the future."

- "An expectation is also a belief that someone will or should achieve something."

You will have had your expectations about where you would live, what your lifestyle would be like, and what your family would be like. An 'expectation' is also a belief that someone will or should achieve something. In marriage, this means that you would also have had a conviction about what your spouse would be like as a husband and father or as a wife and mother. Your expectations aren't just established before your wedding day, they grow, they develop, and they change as the years go on. Your expectations today will be different than the expectations you had years ago.

When you believe something, when you put your trust in something, you expect that it will happen. It moves from something that is a 'perhaps one day' to a 'definitely will' position. This 'belief' is why people treat unmet expectations with the same strength as broken promises. In fact, no promises need to be made for an expectation to be established. In other words, an expectation is something that you have built in your own mind, it can, but it doesn't have to have anything to do with something that someone has led you to believe or promised would happen.

An expectation can be realistic or unrealistic but once it is set it is hard to change. Often couples are too rigid, and their desires are set in stone. It's important that you both examine your expectations and are willing to adjust them. Without adjusting your expectations, you cannot make a fresh start.

The synonyms for the word 'expectation' make it very clear that expectations are not based on facts. There is no hard evidence that your expectations will be fulfilled. Expectations are not established facts, they are not uncontrollable entities, they are manageable, they (the expectations, not the people) are in your control.

SYNONYMS:

- supposition, assumption, presumption, conjecture, surmise, calculation, prediction, hope, anticipation, expectancy, eagerness, excitement, suspense

There are a lot of things though, that are not within your control, you will need to become comfortable with that. You can't control your spouse's behaviour or force them to become someone they are not. Worrying, bullying or keeping your fingers crossed won't change your future but God can.

Everyone Expects Something

We all enter marriage with expectations. There are no exceptions to this. Even when you don't expect marriage to be successful, this also can be categorised as an expectation.

We recently read an article about the expectations of Christian singles. One man articulated his very clear vision of what his intended should be like, "Well, I want a woman who loves the Lord. I want someone who has character and has committed her life to serving Him. I'm really interested in missions, and I want someone with that kind of a selfless heart. But, I also want her to be REALLY hot." That sounds a lot like big expectations! Disappointment is inevitable when you create a fantasy spouse in your head and have to live with a person who is real and has flaws.

I had a lot of hopes and dreams but most centred around the wedding day. I hadn't put much thought into what life would be like after we tied the knot. That didn't mean that expectations weren't there, they were, it only meant that I wasn't conscious of them. My hidden expectations didn't come to the surface until after the wedding. It was then that I realised that I expected Roy to behave a lot like my father.

My Dad is a quiet man, as is Roy. My Dad is a hard worker, as is Roy. There were many similarities between them, and I think that was like a subconscious rudder that steered me in his direction. I admired and loved my father so it made sense that I would choose someone like him.

The hidden expectations came to the surface when Roy didn't live up to them. I don't remember ever thinking, 'Oh, Roy has exceeded my expectations' although when I look back, I can see that in many areas he has. I do remember feeling disappointed when he didn't. Unfortunately the negative was where my focus was drawn, rather than to the positive. It's a tendency that we have both seen in others too.

We all have preconceived ideas about what married life will hold for us and have often built a 'dream' around it. Many marriage expectations are formed while growing up. You will have observed your parents' marriage, the marriages in your wider family, in your culture and eventually among your friends. You will have been influenced by the patterns you have seen in those relationships. Often, subconsciously, it leads to the formation of expectations of your spouse.

In a study, Michael Argyle and Monika Henderson looked at the concept that each culture has its own relationship rules (Michael Argyle, 1986). Everyone entering marriage has assumptions. Those assumptions are primarily based on the society's rules about the conduct between a husband and wife.

"RULES ARE ONE OF THE MOST IMPORTANT COMPONENTS OF RELATIONSHIPS. BY A RULE, I MEAN BEHAVIOUR THAT MOST PEOPLE, (I.E. MOST MEMBERS OF A GROUP, NEIGHBOURHOOD, OR SUB-CULTURE), THINK OR BELIEVE SHOULD BE PERFORMED, OR SHOULD NOT BE PERFORMED."

The study showed that the set of rules vary from culture to culture so it is safe to conclude that in a cross-cultural marriage the expectations of both husband and wife may vary greatly. Since all marriages are to a degree cross-cultural it is safe to say that every home has two people who have an expectation of what each other's role is in marriage. They have been pre-wired with a set of 'rules' which they expect their spouse to live up to.

I wasn't the only one in our relationship who had expectations. Roy also had expectations of me. I was judging him, but he also was judging me by how I measured up to his expectations. His relationship with his mother was rather different than my relationship with my father. In fact, it could be said that Roy chose me because I wasn't like his mother. He wanted someone who was different, someone who would love him unconditionally.

I don't think I was very good at loving unconditionally, in fact, in the early years of our marriage I was quite manipulative. If I gave love, I expected to receive something, if I didn't get love, then I withheld. My idea of loving him was far from the Agape love that the Bible describes.

You might wonder whether the expectations you formed prior to marriage, about marriage, are all that important. Does your upbringing really have an influence on your marriage? The simple answer is that it does.

So take a moment to reflect and remember what you expected of your marriage. Taking that backwards look is more important than you might think because your expectations set the stage for whether you are delighted, contented or disappointed with your relationship. So what did you Expect?

What Were Your Expectations Of:

- Where you would live?

- How many children you would have?

- Your physical health?

- The demands on your time?

- What your love life would be like?

- What your spiritual life would be like?

- What romance would be like in your relationship?

- How your spouse would treat you?

- Did you have any other expectations?

Some of these are general issues about what you expected from marriage, but there are others which are a lot more personal. Be careful not to use this as an opportunity to vent at your spouse. Be careful not to communicate how they have been such a disappointment to you. We'll be learning a lot about how expectations are formed and the difference between a realistic expectation and an unrealistic one. The problem that you perceive to be with your spouse may well be something wrong with your expectation so don't jump the gun!

'EXPECTATION' IS THE

FAULTY TOOL

BY WHICH WE MEASURE

RELATIONSHIPS.

Inaccurate Measurements

If you were building a home would you ever dream of using a spirit level which is broken? Of course not! You want to make sure that you build a house which is sound and won't fall over after a few years. Unfortunately, 'expectation' is the faulty tool by which you have measured your mate. If your spouse falls short by your measure, the tendency is to blame them when you could be using the wrong plumb line.

Matthew 7:1-5 (ESV)
"Judge not, that you be not judged.
For with the judgment you pronounce you will be judged,
and with the measure you use it will be measured to you.
Why do you see the speck that is in your brother's eye,
but do not notice the log that is in your own eye?
Or how can you say to your brother,
'Let me take the speck out of your eye,'
when there is the log in your own eye?
You hypocrite, first take the log out of your own eye,
and then you will see clearly to take the speck out of your brother's eye.

Matthew 7 begins with a warning about judging others. You may not be aware that you are making judgements every day in your marriage. Judgements about how well your husband or wife is performing, opinions about the motives behind their actions. Perhaps you are judging if they are competent or incompetent at cooking, DIY, budgeting or a plethora of other tasks.

It's time to pause so you can answer a major question. Are you a lenient judge or a harsh one? The legal terms used in Matthew paint a courtroom scene. Perhaps you haven't realised that your home can sometimes feel like a courtroom, a hearing room where the judge is as guilty as the accused, perhaps even more so. If you were judged by your spouse in the same way that you judge them would you be content with the verdict?

It's easy to 'see' or focus on the things others do wrong; it isn't so easy to go through the process of self-examination. In marriage, it's easy to focus on all the things your spouse is doing wrong or has left undone, but what about you? Are you guilty of walking around with a 'beam' or a 'log' in your own eye? If you want your marriage to transform, start with examining yourself.

- If your spouse used the same tool, the same expectations, to measure you, how would you measure up? Would you meet their expectations?

- Have you been guilty of being a harsh judge?

- Take time to ask your spouse for forgiveness, for your own failings or judging them.

    You see, I wasn't the only one in our relationship who

had expectations. Roy also had expectations of me. I was judging him, but he also was judging me by how I measured up to his expectations. His relationship with his mother was rather different than my relationship with my father. In fact, it could be said that Roy chose me because I wasn't like his mother. He wanted someone who was different, someone who would love him unconditionally.

I don't think I was very good at loving unconditionally, in fact, in the early years of our marriage I was quite manipulative. If I gave love, I expected to receive something, if I didn't get love I withheld. My idea of loving him was far from the Agape love that the Bible describes.

You might wonder whether the expectations you formed prior to marriage, about marriage, are all that important. Does your upbringing really have an influence on your marriage? The simple answer is that it does.

Just to Clarify:

- We all enter marriage with expectations.

- There are no exceptions to this rule.

- You can expect it to be good, bad or indifferent but it's still an expectation.

- Even if you aren't conscious of your expectations, you will have subconscious ones.

- You usually discover these when you feel disappointed.

- An expectation is not based on fact.

The Formation of Expectations

The Formation of Expectations

For men and women, the fantasy lives that they build up in their heads about marriage can be rather different. They are however formed in similar ways.

The Early Years

Our expectations begin at a very early age. During our childhood between 0-7 years old, we are in what is known as the imprint period. That means that parents are our primary influencers. Whether they were good parents or bad parents, whether they had a wonderful marriage or a terrible one it's from that model that expectations for the future form. That leaves parents with the massive responsibility to get it right! They hand on to the generations which follow a legacy which is not just to do with wealth, but it is a legacy which impacts relationships.

During the period between 0-7, you learn a lot about how to interact with each other, you learn how to solve conflicts, you learn how to express love. You also learn a lot about who you are; you believe the voices that are around you and the expectations they have of you. You will form expectations of your spouse, and you will also form expectations of yourself.

God makes it absolutely clear to parents that they have a huge responsibility. If you have been blessed by Godly loving parents, then they have given you a wonderful gift! It's important though to realise that your spouse may not have been blessed by a Godly model of how marriage should work. Their home environment might have been very different from your own. You both will have been influenced by how your parents handled conflict, demonstrated affection and modelled marriage.

LAINEY:

I have a lot of happy childhood memories. I remember a home filled with laughter, games and quality time. I remember my Dad and Mum being affectionate with each other. It never once entered my mind that they would divorce because I knew they loved God and each other. Unfortunately Roy grew up in a home where his model was separation and then divorce.

If you grew up in a home full of criticism, then it is likely that you will expect yourself to fail. You may have an inbuilt belief that you will never be good enough, that you will never be beautiful enough and that your spouse will find that out sooner or later.

I have often battled with feelings of inadequacy simply because my mother frequently placed upon me expectations that were too high. I was without my father from the age of seven and from that age I had to assume many adult responsibilities. I can imagine how uncomfortable the shepherd boy David must have felt trying to wear Saul's armour! Wearing the cumbersome expectations of others can be devastating. I wasn't just influenced by my parents relationship but by my mother's expectations of me.

The Pre-Teen Years

From the age of 8 years old, we pass into a new phase of life, the modelling stage. It has been described as a time when you 'model' behaviour a little like trying on a new suit of clothes. Those we model can be parents but equally someone in authority who we look up to. Typically we remain in this stage until around the age of 13.

Roy had to 'try on the suit' of an adult way too early! He couldn't possibly live up to the expectations which had been placed upon him. As a result, he automatically expected criticism; he expected others to be disappointed in him. As his wife, I have had to remember that words of affirmation are vital to him and that critical words cripple him. Could this be why Paul gives us the following advice? Ephesians 6:4 NIV Fathers, do not exasperate your children; instead, bring them up in the training and instruction of the Lord.

We want to highlight this because those inner beliefs can destroy a marriage. Those expectations can influence your ability to give and receive love.

The Biblical model is for parents to bless their children, to love and treasure their children, to train children in the way they should go. The reality is that many of you won't have had that type of childhood. Some parents blessed and forgot to train, some trained and forgot to bless, and some did neither!

Many of you have formed expectations, of yourselves, your spouse, and your children which are unhealthy. It's important to take these to God and ask Him to give you a healthy model to follow!

It's a little stereotypical, but there is some degree of truth in the strength of influence that the connections between 'fathers and daughters' and the 'mother and sons' have on a marriage. Often the way in which a person is treated by the parent of the opposite sex sets up an expectation for marriage which is unrealistic.

While it can be said that a father should be the standard against which his daughter will judge men it's destructive if father's raise their daughters to be entitled. 'Entitled' women don't make good wives.

If a dad has a habit of treating his daughter like a princess then that 'princess' might have difficulty adjusting to being a wife. If all she needed to do is blink her eyes and get her way, then she may be surprised when the same tactics don't work on her spouse. Perhaps the father is in a better financial position than her husband, and suddenly all her 'wishes' are not being met. Her expectations are bound for disappointment.

This was certainly true for Susanna, she had been born into a prominent family and had only to ask if she wanted something. She had no experience of keeping a home since someone was paid to do that job. When she married, she hadn't considered that the difference in their backgrounds might be a potential problem. They both went into marriage with an idyllic 'love conquers all' mentality but love didn't seem enough to conquer the disappointment she felt when she realised that they couldn't afford the things that she had previously taken for granted.

Tom felt the weight of her disappointment. It wasn't just in the things that she said but also in the look of discontent that would cloud her face when he had to say 'no' again. He couldn't understand why Susanna was unable to comprehend that they didn't have the money for the things that she demanded. He couldn't understand why she didn't step up to the plate herself, help out with the housework, get a job or do something! He expected a partnership, and she expected a provider.

MOTHERS & SONS

Mothers can be equally as guilty of serving their sons in a way which creates a big problem for their future daughter-in-law! If a son only knows how to be served but has not learned to serve, then many issues arise as soon as he has to cope with the transition from being single to being married. That type of parenting might keep a son tied to his mother's apron strings and make a new bride resentful.

Unfortunately, there can be 'father-daughter' and 'mother-son' issues at the other end of the scale. If parents have been guilty of abandonment or abuse, then another set of issues are brought into married life. Of course if a parent has been guilty of mistreating, abusing, abandoning or rejecting a child then that child will inevitably find it difficult to trust his or her spouse. Their expectation is that at some point in the future their husband or wife will desert them. This makes it difficult for them to fully trust their spouse no matter how trustworthy he or she is.

If your parents were always fighting, were disrespectful to each other, gave each other the silent treatment, got divorced you will have reacted by setting some sort of expectation. Some people worry that marriage may never work and as a result fear creeps in and impacts how they manage conflict. Others vow that they will never be like their parents and are horrified when they find themselves doing the very thing they had made a childhood promise never to do.

God's plan was that sons and daughters should be loved, treasured, protected and at the same time be trained to have Godly character, to be men and women with wisdom and faith.

Teens and Early Twenties
Friends & Enemies

ROY:

It's at this stage that the beliefs of friends impact your expectations of marriage. I was sure that I would not get married until I was close to age 30. This opinion was in some way influenced by conversations that I had had with my peers during my late teens. The general opinion was that once you got married you were tied down, restricted or limited. It wasn't something my friends were aiming for. To be honest most of them wanted 'a good time' without commitment. Once out of their influence, and within the influence of a pretty girl called Lainey my hopes of marrying and expectations during marriage changed significantly.

Peer pressure isn't fun, often it's the thing that forces you into making unwise decisions even though you know that they are dumb. I would love to rewind and do this stage of my life over again, I would make better friendship choices. I spent too much time worrying about what others thought of me and too little time asking God to guide me. My friends had a lot of theories about life and love but when I look back, I can see that they had been reading too many magazines and didn't have a clue either. It took a while to break some bad habits when I got married. I used to score men out of ten as they walked by. This silly superficial assessment of men wasn't healthy in marriage when Roy should have been my only focus.

God's word is full of scriptures which talk about the importance of the friends we choose, but the reality is many of us fall into friendships and don't even make that choice. Too often we absorb the values of others and our expectations become warped. It has been said that after the age of 21 our core values, or beliefs, don't change unless there is a significant emotional event or through effective coaching. We praise God that that 'significant emotional event' can be when we encounter God, and the effective coaching is through God's word.

- What did your childhood teach you about marriage?

- What impression of marriage did you receive from your parents?

- What expectations were formed about marriage during your youth?

- How did your friends view marriage?

- Did that influence your opinion?

- Can you identify any negative influences on your marriage which originate in your formative years?

  - Ask God to show you the areas where you have believed a lie and ask Him to reveal His truth to you.

Promises, Promises!

In addition to being influenced by our childhood years, our role models and our friends, there is one other main influencing factor that impacts our expectations, our spouse! The expectations formed during our early years of development are strong but are more easily dealt with than expectations that have been based on the promises of a spouse. If promises have been made and not kept, they become a collection of little pebbles in your shoe which rub and irritate as you walk through each day of your marriage.

Some promises should never be made; there are just too many variables, and it isn't realistic to guarantee it. You may have promised your spouse the world before you got married only to find it was much harder to deliver on your promise than you expected. You had good intentions but not much chance of ever delivering on your word.

Unfortunately, some promises are little more than lies told in order to 'take the heat off' you in an argument. You haven't meant what you said and hope your spouse forgets that you promised them something. Don't be fooled into thinking it was just a little 'white' lie; lies are lies, and your spouse won't differentiate between them when you tell them. When you make a promise that you don't mean it might provide you with short-term peace but it will create long-term damage to the trust in your relationship.

This is what the Bible has to say about lies.

Leviticus 19:11 (NIV)
" 'Do not steal. " 'Do not lie. " 'Do not deceive one another.

God makes it 100% clear that he doesn't want people to be dishonest! He doesn't just say don't do it, He makes it clear how He feels about lying.

Proverbs 12:22 (NIV)
The LORD detests lying lips,
but he delights in people who are trustworthy.

Just in case you think that honesty is just an Old Testament standard let's look at what the New Testament has to say about it. We are given very specific instructions that lies shouldn't be part of our Christian walk. It's a habit which is part of your old life, not your new one.

Colossians 3:9 (NIV)
Do not lie to each other,
since you have taken off your old self with its practices.

God is 100% reliable, when He makes a promise He keeps it! He should be the example we follow. When we have a CROSS-cultural marriage false promises and lies will no longer be the basis for your marriage relationship. Your word should be reliable. That might mean breaking some old habits, but it's absolutely necessary in order to make a fresh start.

2 Corinthians 1:20 (NIV)

For no matter how many promises God has made, they are "Yes" in Christ.

And so through him the "Amen" is spoken by us to the glory of God.

When God first convicted me (Lainey) about my habit of lying I had a lot of excuses. It was rarely my intent to lie, but I found it was my fall back option when in stressful situations. I didn't like the habit, and I desperately wanted to change, but I found it quite difficult. I asked God to help me, but I didn't expect the challenge that He gave me. When I told a lie it was usually through embarrassment or shame, I really disliked being humiliated! God's challenge was to make sure I returned 'to the scene of my crime' and confess every time I lied. That meant sometimes phoning people back, at other times walking back into an office. The confession would usually go like this.

The challenge God gave me was to make sure I returned 'to the scene of my crime' and confess every time I would mess up. That meant sometimes phoning people back, at other times walking back into an office. The confession would usually go like this. "I'm sorry, I wasn't honest with you. I was a bit embarrassed when you asked me the question, and I made up an excuse. The real reason I wasn't on time was that I hadn't made it a priority. It's totally my responsibility."

Those situations were a painful lesson, but those lessons were learned quickly. It was much more humiliating to confess that I had lied rather than telling the truth from the beginning. If you have an issue with telling lies perhaps this strategy will work for you too. Whatever you do though start making it a priority to put honesty into your relationship.

- Has dishonesty been a pattern in your life?

- How has this affected your relationship?

- Can you identify promises you have broken to your spouse?

    - If so make sure you apologise and ask forgiveness

    - Don't make more empty promises in an effort to make it up to your spouse.

    - Ask God to help you break this negative cycle.

- Have an honest talk about past promises. If you know there are some that will never be fulfilled then it's time to clean the slate and only make promises that you can keep.

Our life is full of brokenness - broken relationships,
broken promises, broken expectations.
How can we live with that brokenness
without becoming bitter and resentful
except by returning again and again
to God's faithful presence in our lives.
- Henri Nouwen

Changing Expectations

Changing Expectations

If you have encountered disappointment and unmet expectations in your relationship it can be difficult to have faith that anything can change. You may have made repeated attempts to have a fresh start and wonder if there is any point trying. Perhaps you have been surrounded by a few friends who like Job's comforters haven't encouraged you to keep going.

We're pretty confident you will have heard the following phrase a few times, 'The leopard can't change his spots'. It originates in Jeremiah 13:23 which is a verse that gives very little hope for transformation. The main point of the verse though is to illustrate that we can't bring about change ourselves. The changes we are talking about today are not through effort or willpower but because of God's power.

Ezekiel 36:26 NIV
I will give you a new heart and put a new spirit in you;
I will remove from you your heart of stone
and give you a heart of flesh.

It's not that this doesn't require effort, it does! The effort is to get closer to Christ so He can change you. It's with His help that you can put in place the essential guidance that the Bible gives regarding living together as husband and wife. This is not about experimenting with different ideas to give your marriage a fresh start but rather about getting back to basics, back to the user's manual when it comes to your marriage relationship.

ROMANS 12:2 NIV
DO NOT CONFORM TO THE PATTERN OF THIS WORLD,
BUT BE TRANSFORMED BY THE RENEWING OF YOUR MIND.
THEN YOU WILL BE ABLE TO TEST AND APPROVE
WHAT GOD'S WILL IS HIS GOOD, PLEASING AND PERFECT WILL.

God takes what is culturally ingrained, the old mindset and renews us so that we can think like Him. For that renewal to happen, it means something different needs to occur in the home. Christ needs to be put back at the centre. That doesn't happen overnight! It takes discipline and spending time together with God. It means exchanging harsh words for loving ones. It means changing your attitude towards your marriage and transforming your actions towards your spouse. To be successful in this requires that your mind is renewed by what God's Word says about your relationship.

EPHESIANS 5:25-26 ESV
HUSBANDS, LOVE YOUR WIVES,
JUST AS CHRIST LOVED THE CHURCH AND GAVE HIMSELF UP FOR HER TO SANCTIFY
HER, CLEANSING HER BY THE WASHING WITH WATER THROUGH THE WORD.

It also should result in your focus being on letting God work on you rather than you trying to work on your spouse.

- Do you recognise your mind needs renewing?

- Do you pray together every day?

- Do you spend time reading the Word of God?

- Do you make room for God in your life?

'When God doesn't do what we want it's not easy;
it never has been, and it never will be.
But faith is the conviction
that God knows more than we do about this life
and he'll get us through it.
Remember, disappointment is caused by unmet expectations.
Disappointment is cured by revamped expectations.'[1]

Max Lucado

---

1   NKJV, The Lucado Life Lessons Study Bible, eBook: Inspirational
Applications for Living Your Faith

Managing Your Expectations

To manage expectations:

"Seek to prevent disappointment by establishing in advance what can realistically be achieved or delivered by a project, undertaking, course of action, etc." Oxford Dictionary.

There are many quotes which spout varied opinions on whether expectations are a good thing or a bad thing. Many of them doom us to ultimate disappointment if we do expect too much and others say we won't get anything unless we expect something.

> "Blessed is he who expects nothing,
> for he shall never be disappointed."
> -Alexander Pope

High expectations, low expectations and unrealistic expectations set marriages up for failure. Unrealistic expectations are countered by a good old fashioned dose of realism; however, realism isn't all that easy to achieve.

It is of vital importance that you both have a realistic expectation of what married life will be like in a cross-cultural marriage. Often couples enter marriage with a dream of what their life will hold only to find the reality is far from what they imagined. Media hype and romance novels fuelled by your own ability to daydream can lead to your bubble bursting in dramatic fashion.

One of the biggest mistakes a couple entering marriage might make, is to have expectations which are unrealistic. It can be said of all marriages of course, but naivety in approaching a cross-cultural marriage can bring about a greater shock when the reality of life hits.

Wearing rose-coloured spectacles regarding living in a new culture, a new country or remaining in your own and integrating your life with that of your foreign spouse is not ideal. If you have been married for a while those spectacles have probably already been removed, you may have replaced them with other glasses but are those other glasses giving you an accurate picture?

Even for those who have been married for many years, there is a fine line to walk. Perhaps your expectations are at the other end of the extreme. Disappointments having reinforced negative expectations of your spouse. Have the spectacles of doom and gloom taken their place? How can you establish sensible expectations? That comes from managing your expectations in marriage and do that you always need to use God's Word as your basis.

There is a good reason for doing this. Because of the hurts and disappointments of the past, it's often tough to re-establish trust in a relationship. Even if the expectations you had were not based on a promise from your spouse you may feel as though they were and that you have somehow been betrayed. God however, is completely trustworthy! His character is impeccable.

NUMBERS 23:19 (ESV)
GOD IS NOT MAN, THAT HE SHOULD LIE,
OR A SON OF MAN, THAT HE SHOULD CHANGE HIS MIND.
HAS HE SAID, AND WILL HE NOT DO IT?
OR HAS HE SPOKEN, AND WILL HE NOT FULFILL IT?

- Was there a specific point when you realised that your spouse wasn't perfect?

- Are you aware of your own imperfections too?

What can Change?

Managing expectations also means you need to understand what is changeable and what isn't. Sometimes we create a wishlist of the things that we would like in our relationship. We have discovered that the wish-lists that are in the hearts and minds of husbands and wives are about as realistic as the checklists they had when they were single! In other words not realistic at all!

Lainey:

When I was single, I had quite a long list. I have to admit to a certain degree of shallowness because I wanted someone tall, handsome with dark hair, dark eyes and a great physique. I dutifully tagged 'Christian' onto the end of the list too and then promptly moved my 'after-thought' to the number one spot. I then thought that it might be a good idea to have someone who was extroverted because they could become a dynamic Christian leader one day.

A quick scan of my list when I met Roy meant that I had to discard some of my ideals. I was relatively content in the assumption that in most of the areas that he failed to meet my criteria I could convince him to change. I could erase dark hair and dark eyes off my list without too much sacrifice but I really struggled with Roy's introversion. It was something that I thought might limit him and I suppose, subconsciously I thought it would have a domino effect and limit me.

"LET'S CLARIFY SOMETHING: THE WORD INTROVERT DOESN'T MEAN SHY OR REMOTE. IT IS AN ENERGY TERM, MEANING THE PERSON'S MAIN SOURCE OF REFUELLING IS GETTING SOME CAVE TIME AND BEING ALONE. BUT INTROVERTS CAN BE FRIENDLY, WARM AND OUTGOING." DR JOHN TOWNSEND

As an extrovert I had the internal believe that my way of doing life was right and that Roy was somehow broken. Unfortunately, I also thought that somehow it was my job to fix him! That involved dragging Roy out to every social event under the sun, it also involved inviting numerous people to our home so Roy could practice socialising. I thought all of these activities would cure him of his introverted tendencies. Do you remember the Albert Einstein quote we used right at the beginning?

"WOMEN MARRY MEN HOPING THEY WILL CHANGE. MEN MARRY WOMEN HOPING THEY WON'T CHANGE. INEVITABLY BOTH WILL BE DISAPPOINTED" ALBERT EINSTEIN

I needed to learn that being introverted is not the same thing as being broken. It wasn't something that needed to be 'fixed' in Roy. Of course, there were areas that did need to change, but this wasn't one of them. Personalities can be judged subjectively; there isn't really a right or wrong just a preference. Character, however, can be judged objectively; there certainly is a right or wrong in behaviour. Character is not another word for personality type.

> "CHARACTER IS YOUR BACKBONE
> WHILE PERSONALITY IS THE ADORNMENT."
> Life For Singles - Lainey Hitchman

Trends today have pushed towards personality being valued more than moral character, we just have to take a look at politics and the movie industry to see this. The 'adornment' though doesn't stand up under pressure. In a relationship you might have all the charisma someone could ever wish for, yet, it would not be enough. You need good character to maintain a relationship.

> "CHARACTER IS THE MORAL AND ETHICAL STRENGTH OF A PERSON.
> IT ISN'T ONLY IMPORTANT TO ACT WITH INTEGRITY
> IN FRONT OF PEOPLE
> BUT A TRUE MEASURE OF YOUR CHARACTER
> IS WHAT YOU DO WHEN YOU THINK PEOPLE ARE NOT LOOKING."
> Life! For Singles - Lainey Hitchman

Character traits include being faithful or unfaithful, honest or dishonest, trustworthy or untrustworthy, brave or cowardly, loving or harsh and responsible or irresponsible. This is by no means an exhaustive list! If you really want to have a fresh start in your marriage, then it is essential that you allow God to work on your character!

Our daughter recently had to go to a chiropractor for some treatment. The first thing that he did was to take an x-ray so he could see if there were any vertebrae that were out of alignment. Once he identified the problem he asked her if she had noticed certain symptoms in her life such as tiredness, headaches and dizziness. He then started to re-adjust the areas which were out of alignment. Although she felt immediate relief, it wasn't a one-time only thing. She was told that she would need to keep coming back for a while until the new position of her spine was established.

You may have been aware of the symptoms but un-aware of the cause of the difficulties you have been walking through as a couple. Understanding the areas of character that need some adjusting is only one step in the process. You then need to ask God to help you work on those areas. You may find that you mess up and slip back into old patterns, that isn't the time for giving up! Keep taking those things back to God and ask Him to help form the character that you need. In time you will see the transformation!

- Have you been guilty of trying to change something which 'isn't broken' in your spouse?

  - Ask your spouse to forgive you.

  - Ask God for a new perspective of your spouse.

- Which character traits do you need to work on?

- Ask God to help you change.

- Keep going until the change is established.

Good character is often the result of good parenting. Good moral values can be taught; they are taught by parents, churches, schools and to a certain degree by society. Godly character though is something that grows and develops rather than something that is static, but it isn't just natural effort which makes this happen. Galatians tells us that it is the fruit of the Spirit of God working in our lives.

Galatians 5:22-23 (ESV)
But the fruit of the Spirit is love, joy, peace, patience, kindness, goodness, faithfulness, gentleness, self-control; against such things there is no law.

The secret to change isn't in observing the law it is in learning to walk by the Spirit. Sometimes, because you want your spouse to change, you might be tempted to lay down the law. You make demands and require them to behave in a certain way. The problem with doing this is that you might end up with a submissive spouse, a compliant spouse but also a resentful spouse.

Most people fall into the trap of trying to change their marriage using all the wrong tactics. They wonder why after all their efforts their marriage is still the same or perhaps even worse. People often reach a point of hopelessness and say that they have tried everything. The 'everything' usually involves every type of manipulation known to man!

Proverbs 19:13 CEV describes what it's like to be under that type of pressure.

"A NAGGING WIFE GOES ON AND ON LIKE THE DRIP, DRIP, DRIP OF THE RAIN."

Manipulation, nagging and bullying will just make your spouse want to move out!

IT IS BETTER TO LIVE IN A CORNER OF THE HOUSETOP THAN IN A HOUSE SHARED WITH A QUARRELSOME WIFE.
PROVERBS 21:9 (ESV)

In Galatians 5:14 We are told that the whole law is fulfilled in one word: "You shall love your neighbour as yourself." God simplifies everything to make it more manageable. He also paints a scene which is prevalent in many homes in verse 15: But if you bite and devour one another, watch out that you are not consumed by one another. Where the fruit of the Spirit isn't present, it is a war zone!

Perhaps this chapter hasn't been applied too often in the area of marriage, and yet it holds an important key to seeing change firstly in you and secondly in your marriage. Win the war within you to win the war in your home! There is a war within you which takes place between the flesh and the spirit. Both pull in opposite directions; both have different desires. To win the war within you, you need to 'walk by the Spirit, and you will not gratify the desires of the flesh'.

"Trade your expectations
for appreciation and
you will see your relationship transform."
-Author Unknown

Changing Attitudes

When you are on the winning side of the war between the Spirit and flesh, you will notice that your attitude starts to change. You will have a lot more grace for one another. It doesn't mean that all of the changes that need to happen occur overnight, but it does mean that transformation is on its way.

Lainey:

My encounter with grace came in an unexpected way, through a pair of Roy's underpants. Unfortunately for Roy, a lot of people know about his underpants. The 'Underpants Story' is one I have told again and again when we have been speaking about marriage. Roy's underpants represented one of my unmet expectations quite simply because I expected him to pick them up and put them in the laundry basket!

It didn't seem like a difficult task, and I remember being puzzled when I found them on the floor each morning. His underpants didn't always 'land' on the same spot. Sometimes they were right beside the bed, sometimes they were at the end of the bed, at times they made it to the door. On occasion, I was surprised to find that his underpants had found their way to a spot 'beside' the laundry basket. They didn't seem to manage to make the jump into the laundry basket though; that was obviously one step too far.

Roy's roaming underpants mildly irritated me to begin with, but as time went on my frustration increased. When I asked Roy about them, he was never quite sure how they got to the place they were because he was sure he had put them away. Over time my attitude changed, for the worse! Picking up his underpants provided me with time each day when I could fume about how someone could be so lazy, so thoughtless, so frustrating! My resentment grew, and I became positive that Roy had concocted some sort of plan to provide me with extra jobs to do each day. The atmosphere in the home became stale.

One day, I finally had the brainwave that I should pray about the problem. If I couldn't change Roy's bad habits, maybe God could. The first day my prayer wasn't much better than my complaining had been. "Dear God, please help Roy to stop leaving his underwear lying everywhere. I don't know why he is so lazy, so inconsiderate ..." and my complaints rolled off my tongue in prayer to God. I realised that had expectations of God too; I expected Him to do as I had asked and change Roy's behaviour. When God didn't 'perform' either I became even more frustrated.

God finally got my attention during one of my prayer 'rants'. I knew He was challenging me to change my attitude, that my attitude was, in fact, a much bigger issue than Roy leaving his underpants on the floor. Roy's underwear might not smell nice but my attitude stank. I started to pray differently than I had before. I began to thank God for Roy, at the beginning that was difficult. It started with "Dear God, thank you that I have a husband who leaves his underpants on the floor". Soon though genuine thanks started to flow and what had been a time of complaint and frustration became a daily time of prayer and thanksgiving. A miracle had happened but it had been in my heart!

- Are there habits which irritate you about your spouse?

  - What is your attitude like to your spouse when they do those things?

  - If you have had a bad attitude ask God for help to change it.

The first book in the Cross-Cultural Marriage Series, Bringing Worlds Together will help you identify behaviours which need to change and those that don't.

Changing Habits

It's possible to draw the wrong conclusion after reading the story of Roy and his underpants, especially if you are the sort of person who tends to get in the bad books because you have habits that your spouse doesn't like. You might think my story illustrates that it's up to your spouse to live with your habit and just change their bad attitude. I have bad news for you; that's not the point I was trying to make.

Roy and I, just like most couples, have habits which irritate each other. Having spilled the beans on one of Roy's bad habits it is only fair to turn the spotlight on one of mine. I am not perfect by any stretch of the imagination. This particular habit dropped into a few categories and was part of my character (which I mistook for my personality), something that originated from my culture.

If you have ever visited Northern Ireland or have some Northern Irish friends, then you probably have realised that sarcasm is ingrained within the culture. Most Northern Irish people have sarcasm running through them just as Blackpool Rock has those words running through it. My humour was cutting, and Roy frequently took the brunt of my comments. I didn't do it to hurt him; I thought I was being funny. When he would get offended, I would accuse him of not having a sense of humour which only added to the wounds. I justified my behaviour by declaring it was 'who I was' and if I tried to change I would be denying that.

Finally, God got my attention. A passage of scripture, that had been read at our wedding, caught my attention.

1 CORINTHIANS 13:4-7 (ESV)
LOVE IS PATIENT AND KIND; LOVE DOES NOT ENVY OR BOAST;
IT IS NOT ARROGANT OR RUDE. IT DOES NOT INSIST ON ITS OWN WAY;
IT IS NOT IRRITABLE OR RESENTFUL; IT DOES NOT REJOICE AT WRONGDOING,
BUT REJOICES WITH THE TRUTH. LOVE BEARS ALL THINGS,
BELIEVES ALL THINGS, HOPES ALL THINGS, ENDURES ALL THINGS.

I realised that I loved myself more than I loved Roy and I wasn't living up to God's definition of love. I needed to change or this would become a problem within our marriage. I don't want you to get the impression that change was easy. It was necessary, but it wasn't easy at all! Daily I asked God to help me change, to renew my mind so that I wouldn't run on old tracks, on old ways of doing things, on old ways of being. I reminded myself of what God had promised.

2 CORINTHIANS 5:17 (ESV)
THEREFORE, IF ANYONE IS IN CHRIST, HE IS A NEW CREATION. THE OLD HAS
PASSED AWAY; BEHOLD, THE NEW HAS COME.

It might be helpful for me to explain the process I went through to change this ingrained behaviour. I encouraged

Roy, to be honest about his feelings whenever I made a cutting remark. Instead of hiding them and putting on a brave face Roy began to admit when he felt hurt. This way I could see the effect of my cutting remarks, the potential for injury and the weakening of our relationship. Each time I would apologise, explain that I didn't mean what I had. I would then go through a process of reassuring Roy and repairing the damage that had been done by my tongue.

Proverbs 14:14 (ESV)
The wisest of women builds her house,
but folly with her own hands tears it down.

I realised that I wasn't tearing down my home with my hands but with my words. I knew that I needed to control my tongue to prevent further damage. Over time the habit lost its power, old patterns fell away as I caught my cutting words before I spoke. Every day I saw more of the old 'pass away', the old habits, the old sarcasm and I didn't miss it!

Roy:

It might seem strange that up until now I had hidden the effect of Lainey's sarcastic nature. If it was a such a big problem, why hadn't I addressed it more directly before then. The truth was that even though I had identified it as a problem, I had thought the problem was all mine. Remember my background, my childhood, my mother's dissatisfaction with my attempts to fulfil responsibilities beyond my maturity.

This had formed part of who I was at that time. Instead of identifying that Lainey's sarcasm was harsh I had thought that I was overly sensitive and I just needed to toughen up a bit. I had drawn the conclusion that sarcasm was normal and my response to it was odd, that cutting words were loving banter and my past hurt left me vulnerable allowing them to cut deep. Until Lainey had realised her words were damaging, and until she had encouraged me to be honest about my feelings, I had failed to recognise that WE (not just me) had a major communication problem in our marriage.

These realisations about our brokenness and our need for change enabled us to move more towards a Christ centred CROSS-cultural marriage. Previously our cross-cultural relationship had resulted in us both being cross and not understanding each other's culture. With God's intervention we started to understand that God had given us both the power to change what was ingrained, that gave us hope!

- Are there things you do which irritate your spouse?

- Are there things you know you need to change?

- What have you done to try and break those habits?

Expectations of Love & Romance

Adam's Expectations

It's normal to have expectations, even Adam, the first man, had expectations of marriage! If any couple had the potential to have a perfect marriage, it was Adam and Eve. We can read their love story in Genesis 2 where it starts with the search for a companion for Adam.

God recognised Adam's need for a companion, "It is not good that the man should be alone; I will make him a helper fit for him." There isn't any dialogue where Adam complains to God that he is lonely, we don't get that sort of detail from the account, but we do find out that God knew it wasn't good for man to be alone. The need for companionship is a basic human need, but God knew he needed more than a friend he needed a wife. When God created Eve, this was one of the aspects that God created her to fulfil.

The second need that Adam had was for someone to help him. It's important that we have a correct understanding of what the word 'helper' means. It's not the word for slave, it's not the word for servant, it's not a derogatory term at all! It's a word that is used 21 times in the Bible. In most cases, it is used in conjunction with words such as shield and deliverance. God wasn't giving Adam the impression of someone who was going to be weak. Can you imagine Adam's excitement as he waited to see who the Lord was going to give him?

I'm sure that as Adam waited his anticipation rose. He already knew the amazing creative abilities of God, and God had promised to make him someone who would be his helper, someone perfectly suitable for him, someone who would be his companion and cure his loneliness. Perhaps you had the same sense of anticipation as you wondered who you would get married to?

THE MAN GAVE
NAMES TO ALL LIVESTOCK AND
TO THE BIRDS OF THE HEAVENS AND TO EVERY
BEAST OF THE FIELD. BUT FOR ADAM THERE WAS

NOT FOUND A HELPER FIT FOR HIM.

SO THE LORD GOD CAUSED A DEEP SLEEP TO FALL UPON THE MAN,
AND WHILE HE SLEPT TOOK ONE OF HIS RIBS AND CLOSED UP ITS
PLACE WITH FLESH. AND THE RIB THAT THE LORD GOD HAD
TAKEN FROM THE MAN

HE MADE INTO A WOMAN

AND BROUGHT HER TO THE MAN.
THEN THE MAN SAID,

"THIS AT LAST

IS BONE OF MY BONES
AND FLESH OF MY FLESH;
SHE SHALL BE CALLED WOMAN,
BECAUSE SHE WAS TAKEN OUT OF MAN."
GENESIS 2:20-23 (ESV)

At Last!

At last! How many of you experienced that feeling on your wedding day? At last! Finally! You could get married to the man or woman of your dreams. It's something you wait for, long for, anticipate, and with each waiting moment your dreams of what it will be like build.

Adam was delighted. He might have thought that he had been given someone just like him! We will never know for sure, but his cry, 'Bone of my bones and flesh of my flesh' certainly gives us that impression. God had created, Eve, his wife, right from his side. Surely you couldn't get anyone more like him if you tried! And yet ... God in his creative genius hadn't just created a clone of Adam he had created a woman who didn't just look different on the outside. She was unique. Similar and yet different. Created in the image of God just like He was but not identical to Adam.

The rib can also be translated as a chamber or a capacity. Adam had capacities and abilities that Eve didn't, and Eve had capacities and abilities that Adam didn't. They would have to learn to work together if they were going to be able to fulfil the task that God had given them. It's clear from the rest of the account in Genesis that it didn't go as smoothly as Adam might have expected. For Adam and Eve, the honeymoon period was over when sin came into the garden of Eden. It brought disappointment, and it brought blame. It also brought hard work!

- Are you still in your 'honeymoon' period?

- Did you enter marriage with a realistic idea of each other's giftings and abilities?

- Do you have a solid friendship with each other?

- Do you find it easy or difficult to work together on projects?

- Has marriage met your need for companionship and help?

- Are you ready to do some hard work to receive the reward of a good marriage?

Expectations of Love

Did You Expect it to be Easy?

Many couples we have spoken to had no idea that marriage would take work. They had a romantic notion that because they were in love and seemed to suit each other so well they would simply run off into the sunset together and live happily ever after. Fairy tales have successfully sold this 'happily ever after' illusion. When reality finally hits, the shock of a relationship needing work, maintenance and effort is hard to swallow.

> "As you become older,
> you become less judgmental and take offense less.
> But marriage is hard work;
> the illusion that you get married
> and live happily ever after is absolute rubbish."
> Julie Andrews

Most stories end where real life begins. Fairy tales don't show you what happened to the prince and princess once they got married. Movies often depict the process of getting together, and the grand finale is when they finally achieve that. Not many stories end with 'and they worked hard to maintain a happy and healthy relationship', do they?

Rather than the happily ever after that so many hope for, many couples end up in the 'they made no effort and were miserable, regretting their decision to marry', category. Some believe it is because they made the wrong choice yet the reality is that all relationships fail when a couple don't work at it. There is no need for any couple to fall into this group! We need to eradicate the lies we believe about marriage and find the truth about how to make it work. Marriage does work; it can bring much joy, and it can last forever, but you can't use a fairy tale recipe to create a real-life happy marriage.

Ecclesiastes 4:9 (NIV)
Two are better than one,
Because they have a good reward for their labour.

Expecting a Soul Mate

What about if you grew up with the belief that the person you marry would be your soulmate? It wouldn't be the first time that we had to work with couples who believed just that! Unfortunately falling for the 'soul mates' lie has led couples to wonder if they made a big mistake. They thought they had found their perfect fit; they thought they had discovered the other half of their soul only to discover that life wasn't that simple.

The soul mates myth is grounded in Greek mythology, it is also the subject of romantic ideology.

"He's more myself than I am.
Whatever our souls are made of,
his and mine are the same."
Emily Brontë, Wuthering Heights

As romantic as it may sound, Heathcliff and Cathy are not the best examples of a healthy relationship. Yet, this myth creeps into the thinking of many Christians. It's important to examine the foundation of your beliefs because what you believe about your relationship will dictate whether it will be successful or if it will fail. The belief that there is only one perfectly suited to you is a dangerous ideology!

According to the Greeks our ancestors had two

heads and four arms. As punishment for offending a God, they were split down the middle, and the human race was created. Therefore according to the legend, we are condemned to spend our lives searching for the other half, our soul mate. In so doing it reinforces the misconception that when you marry your spouse should complete you. That places a tremendous responsibility on your spouse! The only place you can find completeness in Christ, your spouse can that expectation.

The creation story says nothing about God making someone for Adam who was the 'perfect fit' the 'missing piece'. For those expecting a soul mate, double check the scripture, God didn't create your spouse as a soul mate; they are your 'workmate' or 'helpmeet'. Ideology is not the same thing as sound theology.

Adam and Eve were not separated after the garden of Eden, doomed to wander the earth to find each other. However, they were both faced with the reality of having to work at their relationship. They did sin, and they had to live with the consequences of that sin and its impact on their relationship.

The concept of having a soul mate is dangerous because you can mourn a past relationship thinking that person was your only chance at happiness because they were your soul mate. Feeling as though you missed the one can prevent you from fully embracing your spouse.

Another issue is that we can be easily convinced that we married the wrong person if we believe this soul mate lie. As soon as you feel a disconnect or recognise an area of disagreement, it will make you doubt your choice. A good relationship is not one where you are clones of each other. A good relationship is one in which you can celebrate your differences.

What if your spouse dies? If you believe that there is only one possible true love, does it mean that should you remain single? Do you see the problem?

More than one affair has been started as a result of this insidious lie. Commitment is tossed away in the pursuit of an illusion, a hope, a dream of happiness without effort. In our instant world lust is mistaken for love.

The 'soul mates' lie is just one of many that people fall for, they believe it not because they have a fascination with Greek mythology but because it has crept into modern thinking. In fact, that is often the most difficult type of lie to detect; it is so subtle most people haven't even paused to consider why they believe it is true. Few people stop to consider the concept's origins and whether it lines up with what God says about His design for relationships.

We've just taken a look at Adam's expectations in Genesis 2. Right after God presented Eve to Adam there are some crucial instructions that they are given. Remember these are instructions from the designer himself! In one short verse, some of the most important keys to marriage are revealed. It's important not to just skip over them if they don't line up with your culture.

Genesis 2:24 (ESV)
Therefore a man shall leave his
father and his mother
and hold fast to his wife,
and they shall become one flesh.

You will need to leave and cleave (to hold fast). Joining isn't just some supernatural airy-fairy thing. It is something that is active, ongoing and needs maintaining. In other words, it will take effort to stay together. Fitting two pieces of a jigsaw together is not a good analogy for the marriage relationship. The word 'hold fast' is sometimes translated as joined and sometimes translated as cleave or glued to. In this process, the two of you can become one.

MARK 10:6-9 (ESV)
BUT FROM THE BEGINNING OF CREATION,
'GOD MADE THEM MALE AND FEMALE.'
'THEREFORE A MAN SHALL LEAVE HIS FATHER AND MOTHER
AND HOLD FAST TO HIS WIFE, AND THE TWO SHALL BECOME ONE FLESH.'
SO THEY ARE NO LONGER TWO BUT ONE FLESH.
WHAT THEREFORE GOD HAS JOINED TOGETHER,
LET NOT MAN SEPARATE."

The Greeks believed that through the gods' displeasure couples are separated. God does the opposite; He is part of the marriage covenant, and He is active in blending us together. He wasn't thinking 'divorce' when he joined them!

If you have believed the soul mates lie, then you need to release your spouse from that expectation. No-one should have to live under that kind of pressure! They will be under pressure to perform, to always agree, to always understand and that is a very unhealthy expectation.

- If you have had nagging doubts about whether you married your soul mate or not ask God to help you reject that lie.

- Are you ready to commit to doing some hard work?

Did you Expect it to Last Forever?

There are some expectations that are based on fairy stories. Is the concept of love that will last forever yet another one of those tall tales? Having a relationship that will last forever is a real possibility regardless of what the divorce stats are saying, however, today there is a lot of insecurity about entering into marriage. The prenuptial agreement market has understood this, but they don't offer a guarantee of a happy marriage, rather the prenuptial agreement spells out the terms of the end of the relationship. If you enter into a marriage already planning your escape route, it is unlikely to last a lifetime. We aren't saying that making a lifetime commitment to someone isn't scary, but we are saying that it doesn't need to be.

Most people who are engaged say that the reason that they are getting married is that they are in love. Love is the foundation upon which most couples build their lives, yet the love that we expect and the love that God expects in marriage are not usually the same thing. The love that God designed comes with a lifetime guarantee. The chapter of love, 1 Corinthians 13, boasts about the lasting nature of love in verse 8 and verse 13. We are told it never fails and that it lasts forever. We know that God is not a liar, so what do we do with all the couples out there who split up because they fell out of love? What do we do with the couples who are in a loveless relationship?

It all boils down to a fundamental misunderstanding of love. We hear the word love, and we think of attraction, romance, and passionate sex, but when God uses the word love He talks about love on a whole new level! Let's take a look at 1 Corinthians in the Amplified Version to get a better understanding of the promises that God makes.

1 Corinthians 13:13 (AMP)
And now there remain:
faith [abiding trust in God and His promises],
hope [confident expectation of eternal salvation],
love [unselfish love for others growing out of God's love for me],
these three [the choicest graces]; but the greatest of these is love.

When you love each other with agape love, a purely selfless love, then your marriage will not fail. You will both have your needs met, you will both experience joy, and your marriage will last. If you love each other on the 'feelings' level, your feelings will change daily, you will vacillate between love and hate, you will fall in and out of love. This type of love is not abiding, it is limiting.

"We have to stop asking of marriage what God never designed it to give—perfect happiness,
conflict-free living,
and idolatrous obsession,"

Gary Thomas 'Sacred Marriage'.

An Eternal Promise

Marriage is a covenant; it's by design. God uses the word covenant because it implies a very different type of relationship. In marriage the covenant holds together by choice, rather than by feelings. In marriage instead of serving ourselves we serve each other. It's easy to confuse a covenant with the concept of a contract because we lack understanding on the depth of meaning the term covenant holds. A covenant is the deliberate, purposeful holding together in the midst of everything that would try and tear you apart. Every day you choose to keep your word and stand true to your promise to 'hold fast'.

Genesis 2:24 (ESV)
Therefore a man shall leave
his father and his mother
and hold fast to his wife,
and they shall become one flesh.

If you want to have a marriage that will last, you need to make sure you take some fundamental steps.

- Leave your father and mother.

- Hold fast (or cleave) to your spouse.

To make a marriage work you have to do what the

designer says to do. God knows how marriage will work and how it won't work. He clearly spells out where your family loyalty needs to be, and that is with your spouse, not your parents! He also uses the word cleave which is an active word, it's ongoing, not a one-time thing! That is a sticking together through thick and thin.

In Mark 10 Jesus is very clear about the reasons why a marriage sometimes fails. He told the Pharisees it was the result of people's hard hearts. If you want a marriage that will last make sure your heart is soft towards God and towards each other. Jesus also points the Pharisees back to God's original design. God designed marriage to be the on-going 'togetherness' of a couple until the end of their lives.

MARK 10:5-9 (NKJV)
AND JESUS ANSWERED AND SAID TO THEM, "BECAUSE OF THE HARDNESS OF YOUR HEART HE WROTE YOU THIS PRECEPT. BUT FROM THE BEGINNING OF THE CREATION, GOD 'MADE THEM MALE AND FEMALE.' 'FOR THIS REASON A MAN SHALL LEAVE HIS FATHER AND MOTHER AND BE JOINED TO HIS WIFE, AND THE TWO SHALL BECOME ONE FLESH'; SO THEN THEY ARE NO LONGER TWO, BUT ONE FLESH. THEREFORE WHAT GOD HAS JOINED TOGETHER, LET NOT MAN SEPARATE."

When God put you together He expected you to stick together and let nothing, and no-one, come between you.

Expectations of Romance

"There are as many forms of love as there are moments in time."
Jane Austen

Before we explore the topic of romantic expectations it might be best to define what we mean. We have separated out love, romance and intimacy even though they are sometimes confused with each other. Romantic expectations are based on the actions one would expect to accompany love or expressions with the intent of stirring up love.

Perhaps you were hoping for Pepe Le Pew but think that you may have married Elmer Fudd; someone who could never be accused of being romantic. Expectations of romance vary from culture to culture and from person to person. It's natural to conclude that just as each 'people group' have their own language and their own culture, they will also express their love differently and have their own romantic culture. Could it be possible that Elmer Fudd may have been catching, 'Wascally wabbits' as a romantic gesture for his wife? Some will see Pepe Le Pew as romantic others will see him as overbearing. Bottom line some frustrations can occur in a marriage when you don't understand or appreciate the romantic signals, your partner may be sending.

Generally, women have more expectations of

romance than men do. Romance tends to meet an emotional need within women which is why it is held in such high regard. You just need to take a look at the type of literature and the genre of movies which are stereotypically favoured by men and women to get an idea of what is the priority for them. You may have already guessed which area is generally of higher importance to men.

Romantic Heroes

Although it's not the same for everyone, I was able to separate Mr Darcy from real life. I didn't expect Roy to become an 18th-century man of means and start talking as though he had elocution lessons. I did, however, have some expectations which were more ingrained. I told you about how I looked up to my dad and expected Roy to be like him. I don't know if my Mum thinks of my father as a romantic, but I certainly do. My dad regularly came home with flowers for my mother. He has a love of gardening, and his garden has a plethora of beautiful plants and flowers. My Dad would come in from the garden with a bouquet in hand and present them to my Mum, to me it was a beautiful gesture of love.

Roy is not a gardener. Do I need to say more? Roy is not a gardener so he doesn't pick flowers, he rarely thinks to buy flowers, and he doesn't present flowers. Because of my conditioning, Roy is not a romantic. Yet, my wonderful husband always presents me with a cup of coffee in bed in the morning. This gesture I have learned to appreciate as romance but for many years I have to confess that I took it for granted. I was being blessed and didn't recognise it! We can fill our minds so full of 'romantic heroes' that we can fail to recognise the exceptional person that God has put in our lives.

That doesn't mean that there should be no effort to be romantic. If your spouse values romantic gestures your efforts will reap great rewards!

- What expectations have you formed from the media?
  - TV / Movies
  - Magazines
  - Youtube

- What expectations have you formed from your culture?
  - Your parents
  - Your friends
  - Your co-workers

- How satisfied are you with the romance in your relationship?

- Does your spouse believe they can meet your expectation in this area?
  - If your spouse is discouraged because they are never good enough they are highly likely to give up trying!

Unromantic Heroes

Roy:

For example, I am not romantic. I try, but often it comes out wrong or doesn't work at all. I don't naturally think of romantic things and the opportunities to impress Lainey get missed either because I don't recognise the opportunity, just get it wrong, or I am so slow that some other well-meaning individual steals the initiative from me. For example, just before our last anniversary, I had some things all thought out and planned. I wanted to escape with Lainey to a nice hotel for the night. I planned to slip out early in the morning to buy her some flowers, because I know Lainey loves flowers. It took me a long time realise it! In fact, it took me reading this book to understand just how important it is to her. So, that was my plan; it sounds like a good one doesn't it!

The reality was that somehow I managed to book the hotel for nine months after the event. The credit for the flowers which, I would like to remind you, I had managed to think of all by myself was stolen from me! My well-meaning daughter suggested out loud in front of Lainey that I should buy her flowers. Do you get the picture?

As I said, I am not *naturally* romantic. However, that does not mean that I don't love my wife! I demonstrate my love for her in many ways: a cup of coffee in bed (every morning), I help around the house with housework often!

And although none of these things can be considered romantic or sexy we have to realise that they are loving. If all of Lainey's expectations of love were romantic expectations, she would feel very unloved in this relationship.

By the way, some insight just for the men, I have discovered the secret of romance. Candles! The more, the better. If you want a romantic evening (correction, if your wife wants a romantic evening), you no longer have to dive into a panic racking your brain thinking of what to do. Just reach for the matches and light the candles, put on a chick flick and the problem is solved! It really works too! Now I have so many candles in our living room that when I light them all the temperature in the room goes up several degrees and we have to put on our sunglasses!

Lainey:

Men, I hope you see the humour in this. Roy, I really hope it's not a serious suggestion! Women, if your husband does try this at least give him credit for trying. Remember: An unromantic hero is someone who isn't romantic naturally but makes an effort.

- So what are your expectations of love? Are they realistic?

- How does your spouse express their love to you?

- How do you show your spouse that you love them?

Love is a command, not just a feeling.
Somehow, in the romantic world of music and theater
we have made love to be what it is not.
We have so mixed it with beauty and charm
and sensuality and contact that
we have robbed it of its higher call
of cherishing and nurturing.

Ravi Zacharias

Expectations of Intimacy

Just as you had expectations of love and romance, you also entered marriage with expectations of what your sex life would be like. Those ideas are formed in much the same way as others; you are influenced by the society you grew up in, by your family and friends, by the media and by your faith.

Our first realisation that our expectations in this area might be wrong was on our wedding night. The run up to the wedding had been pretty hectic with late nights and early mornings spent in preparation for the 'big day'. The preparation for the 'big night' didn't include a discussion; it didn't include taking exhaustion into account. I had however bought some lingerie, so I felt well prepared.

The day was beautiful, busy, emotional and intense. We left the wedding reception with a sense of accomplishment; we were finally married! We drove away with tin cans trailing behind us and a car decorated well enough to draw attention to the newly-weds. Then a flood of emotions hit me. Poor Roy sat bewildered as I cried. I'm sure he wondered if he had somehow 'broken me' and what he needed to do to 'fix me'. When we went to the hotel I had the urge to cry rather than the urge to make love. No one had warned us that might be the case.

I think we both spent our wedding night frustrated by the circumstances. Our expectations had not been met. When your expectations are higher than what is realistic you will inevitably be disappointed in your relationship. It's a formula which always has the same result.

$$\text{DISAPPOINTMENT} = \frac{\text{EXPECTATION}}{\text{REALITY}}$$

- What were your expectations of intimacy before marriage?

- Were your expectations similar or different?

- Were those expectations realistic or unrealistic?

Sex was designed by God to be a wonderful blessing in marriage. He designed intimacy to be fulfilling and life-giving, but many couples have experienced disappointment because of false expectations. Those expectations have been built on a brittle web of lies, and yet many people are surprised when they are disappointed. They miss the true joy of sex because they haven't understood how God designed it. This lie is as destructive as the other.

"BECAUSE MOST MEN AND WOMEN HAVE DIFFERING IDEAS,
STANDARDS, AND EXPECTATIONS ABOUT SEX,
IT'S NO WONDER THAT MANY MARRIAGES SUFFER IN THIS AREA".
-DENNIS AND BARBARA RAINEY

HALF-HEARTED & HARD-HEARTED

Unfortunately instead of the passionate experience that many couples expect, some end up in half-hearted instead of heated responses to each other. That is demoralising, to say the least! There is nothing quite like feeling that your spouse desires you. There is nothing quite like the feeling of rejection you receive when your advances are met with distaste or lack of enthusiasm. Ephesians 4 sheds some light on why this type of half-hearted response happens. It seems that the issue isn't so much that of having deaf ears, but of having a hard heart.

EPHESIANS 4:18-20 (ESV)
THEY ARE DARKENED IN THEIR UNDERSTANDING,
ALIENATED FROM THE LIFE OF GOD BECAUSE OF THE IGNORANCE THAT IS IN THEM, DUE TO THEIR HARDNESS OF HEART. THEY HAVE BECOME CALLOUS AND HAVE GIVEN THEMSELVES UP TO SENSUALITY, GREEDY TO PRACTICE EVERY KIND OF IMPURITY. BUT THAT IS NOT THE WAY YOU LEARNED CHRIST!

Without Christ, we all have heart disease. Our hearts become hard and callous, and that affects the responses we have to others. If you are not responding correctly to your spouse in the area of intimacy, check your heart condition. Just to spell it out, the word callous comes from the the Greek word **pōros** which is a kind of marble. If you are cold, unfeeling and unsympathetic to your spouse, then you are experiencing this problem. These are indicators of a heart condition! Perhaps you need a spiritual cardiogram? A cardiogram checks for any abnormalities in the heart. You can have abnormal expectations of intimacy because of your past.

- Has your love grown cold?

- Do you struggle to think about your spouse's feelings?

- Which do you desire more, to please your spouse or be pleased?

- Do you feel loved and cherished by your spouse during love-making?

- How frequently do you make love?

Just as there are many reasons why someone may have problems with their physical heart there may be many reasons why someone struggles in this area. Health issues may also be a huge factor in your spouse's ability to respond, hormone problems or stress can be particularly problematic. It's important to be able to differentiate between a cold-hearted response and an issue caused by ill health.

Snake-Oil

You know that something isn't right when your physical body shows signs of sickness, similarly your marriage can also show signs of weakness. If you are ill, the doctor will usually run some tests to see what's going on. A good doctor will treat the source of the problem while a poor doctor will give you medicine to mask the symptoms.

In the area of intimacy, many people self-medicate instead of getting the problem dealt with at the source. Just as Quacks peddled 'snake oil' in the past with a cure-everything promise, Satan has fooled a lot of people in the area of intimacy. Quacks fake expertise in the medical arena, Satan fakes expertise in the area of intimacy.

Pornography, fantasy, adultery, emotional affairs and masturbation are some of the poisonous array of 'snake-oils' Satan puts on offer. Many people are enticed by the promises he makes only to fall into addictive behaviours which only serve to make matters worse. The dependency created by false intimacy actually makes the heart condition worse instead of better.

The source of the problem is often the lies which create unrealistic expectations. The treatment is a regular dosage of truth.

False Expectations

Part of the issue with the lies which people believe is that they have swallowed them for a long time. Pornography sets a false expectation of performance in a relationship. It sells the idea that if you are good at having sex it equates to a good relationship. Pornography ignores the elephant in the room that sex and intimacy are not synonymous.

Pornography 'sells' self-satisfaction but fails to inform you of the side effects. Fight the New Drug[1] reports that "The more pornography a person consumes, the harder it becomes for them to be aroused by a real person or a real relationship. As a result, many users start feeling like something's wrong with them; they don't know how to be turned on by a real person, much less form a deep personal connection with one." In other words, pornography is not a harmless activity; it harms you!

This particular 'snake oil' has also been sold as something to spice up your sex life with your spouse. It's been marketed as a 'fix' for a boring sex life yet the facts negate the claims. The bottom line is that pornography robs marriage of intimacy, satisfaction and fulfilment. As the lie that pornography is not harmful is digested it poisons the consumer and damages their relationships. 2-in-2-1[2]

---

1   fightthenewdrug.org/
2   2-in-2-1.com

collated information regarding the truth behind the porn lie. With double the risk of divorce, dissatisfaction is a symptom of this type of viewing. This is especially evident when women view pornography, they are three times more likely to become discontent with their spouse.

Do you think there would there be as many sales if the truth were known? Unlike medicine or cigarettes, pornography has no warning label other than that of graphic content. Smoking can kill, pornography can kill a relationship.

"I HAVE ALSO SEEN IN MY CLINICAL EXPERIENCE THAT PORNOGRAPHY **DAMAGE**S THE **SEXUAL PERFORMANCE** OF THE VIEWERS. PORNOGRAPHY VIEWERS TEND TO HAVE PROBLEMS WITH PREMATURE EJACULATION AND ERECTILE DYSFUNCTION. HAVING SPENT SO MUCH TIME IN **UNNATURAL** SEXUAL EXPERIENCES WITH **PAPER, CELLULOID** AND **CYBERSPACE,** THEY SEEM TO FIND IT **DIFFICULT** TO HAVE SEX **WITH A REAL HUMAN BEING.** PORNOGRAPHY IS **RAISING THEIR EXPECTATION** AND DEMAND FOR TYPES AND AMOUNTS OF SEXUAL EXPERIENCES; AT THE SAME TIME IT IS **REDUCING THEIR ABILITY TO EXPERIENCE SEX.**"

– DR. MARYANNE LAYDEN[3]

3   Reisman, Sanitover, Layden, and Weaver, "Hearing."

- Have you or your spouse viewed pornography?

  - How has it affected your appreciation of your spouse?

- Are both of you satisfied when you make love?

  - Do either of you feel dirty, defiled or degraded when you have sex?

- How has it affected your ability to be intimate?

  - Physically

  - Emotionally

  - Spiritually

- Do you recognise any false expectations in the area of intimacy?

False expectations in the area of intimacy are not only created by pornography. There are other sources which many people have given credibility, yet they too are often inaccurate.

Unfortunately many Christians in an effort to keep their children pure misinform them about sex. It is painted as something base and carnal rather than something to be enjoyed. Those who have believed this lie have been robbed of a beautiful gift.

WHO TOLD YOU THAT?

GENESIS 3:11 (ESV) HE SAID, "WHO TOLD YOU THAT YOU WERE NAKED? HAVE YOU EATEN OF THE TREE OF WHICH I COMMANDED YOU NOT TO EAT?"

When sin entered the world, there were a number of consequences. One of the first things we see Adam and Eve doing is hiding and trying to cover up. They were ashamed, and that shame created a barrier between them and God. It wasn't that God didn't know what they had done, but they didn't feel as though they could approach God. When they finally talk to God about what happened God asks an important question, 'Who told you?'

In the area of expectations, it's a good question to ask. 'Who told you what to expect'? Often the information we receive is not correct or not the whole truth. Ephesians 4 has a lot to say about how we often live life in ignorance and how that prevents us from living life as God intended. The area of intimacy is no exception!

- Where did the expectation originate? It's important to identify the source of your expectations:

  - Culture

  - Friends

  - Home

- Day Dreams

- Media

- Books

- Pornography

You have to ask yourself where did that idea come from? Who told you that? It's not that everything that you have heard about sex is a lie, but some of it might be. So how do you know what is a lie and what is the truth? How do you know when you have set up an expectation which isn't correct? You have been influenced, you have formed your expectations of marriage but what are those expectations. The expectations aren't just from your family and friendship circle, but they have also been moulded by the culture and the media.

It's important that you have the right source of information! It's also vital that it lines up with the Word of God. Jesus warns us in John 8:44 about Satan's character, that he is a liar and the father of lies so we need to be careful who we let have a voice into our lives.

YOU ARE OF YOUR FATHER THE DEVIL, AND YOUR WILL IS TO DO YOUR FATHER'S DESIRES. HE WAS A MURDERER FROM THE BEGINNING, AND DOES NOT STAND IN THE TRUTH, BECAUSE THERE IS NO TRUTH IN HIM. WHEN HE LIES, HE SPEAKS OUT OF HIS OWN CHARACTER, FOR HE IS A LIAR AND THE FATHER OF LIES.

What Does God Know About Sex?

"If you want to know how to have a great sex life, then you need to find out what God says about it." Roy and I glanced over at the couple we were counselling and saw a familiar reaction. The wife immediately went a dark shade of red and found that her handbag was suddenly very interesting. Simultaneously the husband's eyebrows raised in disbelief as he blurted out, "Seriously?" With the realisation that we were indeed serious sweat appeared on his upper lip, and he paled.

If you want to know the truth about how to have a great sex life, then ask God. For some reason, many people really struggle with this. They have a 'What would He know?' attitude. Yet, God designed us and knows exactly how he created us to respond to each other. Unfortunately, we see a trend to reject God's opinion as people try and figure it out for themselves.

Romans 1:21 (ESV)
For although they knew God, t
hey did not honour him as God
or give thanks to him,
but they became futile in their thinking,
and their foolish hearts were darkened.

These people knew God, but they didn't honour him. There is a big difference between acknowledging that God is real and making him Lord of your life. In the case of the Romans, they thought that they knew better. 'Claiming to be wise, they became fools'. Their 'hearts were darkened' is a metaphor for being unable to see or understand the truth.

Essentially when you know God but don't honour him you get stuck believing a lie. These lies are especially damaging to your relationship because you are convinced that you are doing the right thing. This chapter of Romans talks a lot about idolatry, a lot of modern day idolatry is the worship of self. Pride might be the biggest obstacles you will face in the process of transformation. If you want to understand God's plan for marriage, you will need to lay down your preconceived ideas and be open to seeing things from the Designer's perspective. After all, we are not the experts; God is!

It's surprising how much God has to say about sex, and it's not all, 'Thou shalt nots'. The word 'sex' however is limited in its description of what God had in mind, the word 'intimacy' captures it more thoroughly. The Old Testament euphemism for sex was to 'know' and in many aspects, it's a good description of what God wanted us to experience. Sex describes the physical action, but it should be something that allows us to 'know' each other - body, soul and spirit.

God's Design for Intimacy

1. Fun.

God designed sex to be enjoyed, to be fun! It isn't a gift that is meant to sit on a shelf and only be appreciated on special occasions. It gets better the more you use it! God wants you to 'delight' in each other. He designed it so that you could both enjoy it rather than endure it.

Proverbs 5:18-19 (ESV)
Let your fountain be blessed,
and rejoice in the wife of your youth, a lovely deer, a graceful doe.
Let her breasts fill you at all times with delight;
be intoxicated always in her love.

Unfortunately, in some cultures, the emphasis has been on the man fulfilling his needs with little consideration for the wife. God didn't design sex just for man's pleasure He designed it so that both husband and wife could have fun.

Song of Songs 5:4 (NIV)
"My beloved thrust his hand through the latch-opening; my heart began to pound for him."

This is the type of intimacy where adrenaline kicks in when you know you are going to be together! It's not boring, stale or stagnant.

2. Fulfilling.

God designed sex to be satisfying, to fulfil each of you. Let's make sure we emphasise that - both of you! Instead of expecting to receive pleasure go into lovemaking expecting to please. Make it your goal! Instead of expecting to get, expect to give, and give abundantly because your husband or wife deserves it! One of the reasons that we prefer to use the word intimacy rather than sex is that it more accurately portrays the fullness of the love that God wanted His creation to experience during lovemaking. He designed it to be an experience which is fulfilling - body, soul and spirit.

The Bible uses lots of imagery to describe the fulfilment that intimacy brings, especially that of water. Fountain and cisterns have a meaning which is much deeper than simply talking about a water supply. Proverbs 5 is a good example of this.

Proverbs 5:15-18 (NKJV)
Drink water from your own cistern,
And running water from your own well.
Should your fountains be dispersed abroad,
Streams of water in the streets? Let them be only your own,
And not for strangers with you.
Let your fountain be blessed,
And rejoice with the wife of your youth.

3. Faithful.

The same scripture we have just looked at also warns of the need to be faithful. God designed marriage to be monogamous. He expects you to be faithful. That's being faithful emotionally, mentally and physically!

God designed sex as something that strengthens your commitment to one another. Without getting into the neuroscience of lovemaking, the very act of making love, the physical closeness of a husband and wife causes neurohormones to be released that cause you to be drawn together emotionally. Sexual intimacy within marriage helps cement you together in your relationship.

Your intimacy isn't something that you should take for granted. It is something that you should respect and protect. The book of Hebrews points out that purity isn't something that is just for the single person. So what does that mean? Purity obviously doesn't mean abstinence in the marriage context; purity means the absence of sexual sin. The following verse clarifies that there should be no room for adultery.

Hebrews 13:4 (NIV)
Marriage should be honoured by all, and the marriage bed kept pure, for God will judge the adulterer and all the sexually immoral.

Jesus clarifies in the book of Matthew that this purity is much more than on the physical level, it's also important to be mentally pure in marriage. It's a really high standard to live by, but it will lead to a more fulfilled sex life in marriage.

Matthew 5:28 (NIV)
But I tell you that anyone who looks at a woman lustfully has already committed adultery with her in his heart.

That means being careful about where your focus is, being careful not to let your mind wander to what sex would be like with someone other than your spouse. It means not rating other people as they walk by and not lusting after the latest Hollywood heartthrob.

Sometimes we have been asked if an emotional affair really is an affair. It is! Don't be fooled that just because you don't act upon your thoughts they don't count. There is an old saying that where your mind goes your body will follow. Don't let it lead you into any form of adultery. In fact statistically half of all emotional affairs become sexual affairs[4].

Remember intimacy isn't just on the physical level, you should be intimate on the spiritual and emotional level too. If you are feeling emotionally distant from your spouse, don't fall into the trap of thinking that sharing with someone

---

4   Harrar, Sari and Rita DeMaria. 2007. The 7 Stages of Marriage: Laughter, Intimacy, and Passion. Pleasantville, NY: Reader's Digest Books.

else on an emotional level is okay, it's not. This kind of emotional intimacy should be preserved for your spouse. In Titus 2, older women are told to teach the younger women how to love their spouse. The word used for love in Greek is Phileo; that is the close friendship type of love. Other words for this type of love include: closeness, bonded, connected, communication, support, sharing, feelings, and warmth. Intimacy is designed to touch your heart not just bring you physical pleasure. You need to be emotionally intimate not just physically intimate.

4. FRUITFUL.

God designed sex so it would be fruitful. The purpose of sex isn't solely to have children, but it certainly is one of the by-products. However, sexual fruitfulness is not limited to having children, sex was designed to bring life to your marriage. The old lie that it is for procreation only has robbed many people of life in their relationship.

GENESIS 1:28 (ESV)
"AND GOD BLESSED THEM. AND GOD SAID TO THEM, "BE FRUITFUL AND MULTIPLY AND FILL THE EARTH AND SUBDUE IT, AND HAVE DOMINION OVER THE FISH OF THE SEA AND OVER THE BIRDS OF THE HEAVENS AND OVER EVERY LIVING THING THAT MOVES ON THE EARTH."

You shouldn't stop being intimate because your childbearing years are over. Having children is not the sole purpose for sex. If you have been unable to have children, or you are now too old to have children, you can, and should, continue to enjoy the special gift that God has given of each other's love.

There is a lot of scientific proof that there are many benefits to lovemaking. It benefits your emotional health as well as your physical health. Recent studies have shown that frequent sex improves your immune system, that's a lot more fun than taking vitamins! Oxytocin, which is produced when you make love, also is a bonding hormone which strengthens your relationship. If you're struggling with your libido lovemaking actually helps increase your desire for your spouse, especially if it's regular. It eases stress, lowers your blood pressure, reduces the risk of a heart attack, and improves sleep! It is, therefore, no exaggeration to say that intimacy is fruitful.

5. FREQUENT.

Sometimes we are asked how frequently a couple should make love. Of course, there are many factors involved, and age and stage of life plays a part in your desire. Our best guess is that's it's more often than you might think! 1 Corinthians tells us that if you aren't going to make love, then it should be for a limited time. It also gives the reason for such abstinence, a time devoted to praying!

1 Corinthians 7:5 (ESV)

"Do not deprive one another, except perhaps by agreement for a limited time, that you may devote yourselves to prayer; but then come together again, so that Satan may not tempt you because of your lack of self-control."

That doesn't fall into the category of watching TV or surfing the internet. In fact, one of our top tips is to get rid of the television and media devices from the bedroom. Apparently, the distraction reduces your potential for making love by 50%!

We've often been asked 'How frequent is frequent?', it's a good question! It's difficult to give an answer without first mentioning that there are some considerations you need to bear in mind including stage of life, hormone levels and health. It might be a good time though to reflect on what you are hoping our answer will be. Some people would like to have sex much more than they are at the moment and others are hoping that they can have a lot less!

In 1 Corinthians 7:5 the importance of making love often is stressed. It was never meant to be read as a verse which spouses can use to 'demand' their conjugal rights. It was written as a verse to warn that if you neglect this area of your relationship, you will give the enemy an opportunity to tempt you. If you are struggling to be intimate with your spouse, then it's important that you don't ignore the problem. It won't simply go away.

Find out what the source of the problem is. Whether the issue between you is physical, spiritual or emotional, make sure you get help!

Turn expectations into gratefulness. Instead of having high and unrealistic expectations regarding sex be grateful for each other's company. Rejoice in the fact that you have each other. Ask God to teach you how to make sex satisfying to both of you. God doesn't want you to be flailing in the areas of love, romance and intimacy. He created you, and He wants you to be successful in your relationship.

In the area of intimacy how close to God's design have you been living? Score yourself in the following areas with 0 being the furthermost away from God's plan and 5 being the closest to His design.

FUN   0   5
_____

FULFILLING 0   5
_____

FAITHFUL   0   5
_____

FRUITFUL   0   5
_____

FREQUENT   0   5
_____

WHAT DOES GOD EXPECT?

God Expects Us to Walk In Love

You have already learned that the key to change in our relationship is learning to walk in the Spirit. It's worth pausing and remembering this so that as you learn about God's expectations you don't start falling back into performance mode. Everything you need to make your marriage work doesn't rest on your own ability, it rests in God's ability. He is a covenant partner in your relationship! It does require obedience, but that obedience comes through His strength.

1 John 4:8 (ESV)
Anyone who does not love does not know God,
because God is love.

This verse might seem a little harsh, but it holds an important key to giving your marriage a fresh start. If you are struggling to love then get close to God. Self-help books and magazines are not going to be the source which will help you turn around your marriage. They may give some good psychological advice, but they won't help you as much as the one who designed you and knows you intricately. His nature is that of love, and He will teach you how to love each other well. He is the best example that you could ever follow!

1 John 4:19 (ESV)
We love because He first loved us.

God expects you to love as He loves, selflessly, unconditionally, faithfully, and eternally. There have been days when Roy and I have had to rely heavily on God to give us that love for one another. You know those sort of days when everything you do or say irritates. On those days you have a choice, you can continue getting more and more annoyed with one another, or you can stop and ask God for his help. Some people may mutter irreverently under their breath "God give me strength" but both Roy and I have had times when we have prayed that in all sincerity. The reality is that there are some days when it is not easy to love each other.

The words of Ephesians 5 are reminiscent of God's challenge to walk in the Spirit, this time, His challenge is to walk in love.

Ephesians 5: 1-2 (NKJV)
Walk in Love
Therefore be imitators of God as dear children.
And walk in love, as Christ also has loved us
and given Himself for us,
an offering and a sacrifice to God
for a sweet-smelling aroma.

Many people understand that they have to show Christ-like love to others and do a great job of doing just that. However, these verses were also to be applied to your marriage and to your family. God wants you to care for each other, as husband and wife, in such a way that you will be an example to others. God expects you to have a relationship that reflects His love.

Have you ever wondered if the words offering and sacrifice in this verse are referring to Christ's sacrifice or to ours in choosing to walk in love? I've often observed when a couple love each other the atmosphere around them is sweet, but when a couple is at war with one another the opposite is true. Your witness isn't just with the words you share, it's with the example you set.

John 13:35 (ESV)
By this all people will know that you are my disciples, if you have love for one another."

- What is the general atmosphere in your home like?

- Do you feel like you are walking on eggshells?

- Do you feel welcome in your own home?

- How does your mood influence the mood of your spouse?

- Have you been walking in love towards your spouse?

In Ephesians 5:25 Paul encourages husbands to follow the example of Jesus. He is the ultimate example of true love!

In order to walk in love, it's necessary to gain a deeper understanding of what love is. 1 Corinthians 13:4-8 isn't just a few pretty verses to be read during wedding ceremonies, there is a lot that you can learn in these four short verses about love. If you apply them to your marriage, then you will start to see it transform! Marriage is the place in which you get to practice love, develop love and grow in love. Don't give up!

God Expects You to Grow Together

Roy:

I often say that Lainey is the agent of the Holy Spirit within my life. This doesn't mean that Lainey tries to be everything that the Holy Spirit is meant to be for me, but rather that God often uses her to show me where my character is lacking. Often she does this effortlessly as we live life together. She has this ability to simply burst my bubbles of self-image by pushing buttons that provoke ungodly responses from me. It's not a malicious thing; it's not something she does to "get at me" even. It is just something that happens and is useful to remind me that I am not the super spiritual, ultra-patient, self-disciplined individual that I would have myself believe me to be.

Lainey knows me well. Lainey knows my weaknesses, and the Holy Spirit through Lainey is able to bring me to an understanding that I still need God to help me develop the fruit of the Spirit within my life. I get the privilege of doing this for Lainey also. In fact, I think I am somewhat better at pushing Lainey's buttons.

Why do I say this? Simply to point out that if we find ourselves becoming annoyed at our spouse, at what they do, what they don't do, their timing (or lack of it), their lack of reason; then it is probably better for us to ask why am I getting so annoyed? Why do I need her to do everything my way?

Rather than allow the devil to use these feelings to tear you apart and damage your marriage, the better thing is to allow the Holy Spirit to show you something about yourself. Allow Him to develop your character into being something more Christ-like. Allow God to work on you instead of becoming annoyed with your spouse; you won't regret it!

When your spouse pushes those buttons in you, use it as an opportunity to discover the areas that you need to develop.

- What tests your patience the most?

- Why does that action annoy you?

- Is it something that needs to change in your spouse, in yourself or in both of you?

- Is there something you need to change about your response to your spouse?

WE EXPECT THAT GOD PUT US TOGETHER
FOR OUR HAPPINESS INSTEAD
OF OUR DEVELOPMENT.

God Expects You to Study

God's expectations of how we should behave towards each other in marriage are no secret. There are a lot of verses dedicated to the marriage relationship and to our relationships with others in general. A lot of what Roy and I have learned about marriage has come from reading the Bible and letting God catch our attention. Try making it a habit of reading together and seeing what God shows you about His design for your relationship!

2 Timothy 2:15 (Amp)
Study and be eager and do your utmost
to present yourself to God approved (tested by trial),
a workman who has no cause to be ashamed,
correctly analyzing and accurately dividing
[rightly handling and skillfully teaching]
the Word of Truth.

We specifically chose this version to highlight some important elements. It's not enough to read the Bible at a superficial level. It's important to really understand it, and how to apply it. Unfortunately, over the years, we have encountered incidents when the Bible has been wielded as a weapon against a spouse. The person quoting scripture sounds like they know what they are talking about, but they are taking the Word of God out of context or twisting it.

Really studying God's Word will prevent it from being incorrectly applied, it should also lead to you applying the principles correctly.

- Do you have a time every day when you read the Bible together?

  - How much do you read?

  - Do you discuss it together?

  - Do you apply what you read to your lives?

- Do you pray together?

  - How frequently?

  - How long for?

  - What do you pray for?

The problem is that even if you know a lot, or understand a lot, it won't be enough unless you actually put the principles into practice.

God Expects You to Apply

James 1:22 (NIV)
Do not merely listen to the word,
and so deceive yourselves. Do what it says.

It's too easy to deceive yourselves with phrases like, "My spouse knows I love them." yet, your spouse has been frustrated because you haven't been putting into action the things that you know to do. Perhaps you have been dragged to a number of marriage events or been forced to read some marriage books so you know all the theory. Taking it, applying it, and establishing a pattern is much more difficult. Unfortunately, you may have expected a quick fix only to find out that marriage is hard work.

Of all the expectations that we have looked at, there is a set of expectations that you must endeavour to implement within your relationship and those are God's expectations for your marriage. Working hard to implement these will mean that God's expectations will work hard on you, changing you to be more like Jesus.

We have often been challenged in our marriage with Biblical principles which are not applicable to marriage in an obvious way. I (Lainey) remember God grabbing our attention with the story of Naaman in a way which transformed our marriage. For those of you who aren't familiar with the story, here it is in a nutshell. Naaman was a pretty powerful man, a commander, someone who was more used to giving the orders than getting them. He had one issue though which impacted his life and his relationships; he had leprosy. One of his servants told him that she knew a man who could cure him of the disease. Naaman was willing to pay any price to get rid of his leprosy; it was worth the investment.

Naaman had a lot of expectations about how he was going to get healed. He had found out from the King of Israel that Elisha was the man to see. He went to Elisha's home, but instead of coming out to greet this important man Elisha sent his servant to meet him. To add insult to injury Elisha sent the instruction that Naaman should wash in the Jordan river. This was not what Naaman expected!

2 Kings 5:11-12 (NIV)

But Naaman went away angry and said, "I thought that he would surely come out to me and stand and call on the name of the Lord his God, wave his hand over the spot and cure me of my leprosy. Are not Abana and Pharpar, the rivers of Damascus, better than all the waters of Israel? Couldn't I wash in them and be cleansed?" So he turned and went off in a rage.

Elisha's instruction had injured Naaman's pride. It's worth remembering that Naaman was willing to invest financially in his healing yet he struggled to humble himself to follow through on a basic instruction. Thankfully Naaman finally came around and did what God said, the result was complete healing.

We've met many people over the years who are hoping that God will wave His hand over their marriage so that it can be miraculously healed. They even believe that God has failed them because they haven't been healed yet. We believe in many cases it comes down to a pride issue. They aren't willing to implement the simple things that God has told them to do. They are waiting for a miracle while God wants to do a miracle in them and change their heart.

- Are there things you know to do in your relationship which you haven't been doing?

- What are the principles you already know which you need to start applying?

- If you have been stubborn and resistant to what God has asked you to put in place, ask His forgiveness.

- Start doing what you know to do!

It would be impossible to love selflessly without having some success at putting your selfish nature to death. This remains true regardless of whether you are rich or poor, healthy or battling sickness, or enjoying good or difficult times. It takes a relationship with Jesus to have the strength to be content, whatever your life situations, and continue to be faithful to your wedding vows.

PHILIPPIANS 4:11-13 (ESV)
NOT THAT I AM SPEAKING OF BEING IN NEED,
FOR I HAVE LEARNED IN WHATEVER SITUATION
I AM TO BE CONTENT.
I KNOW HOW TO BE BROUGHT LOW,
AND I KNOW HOW TO ABOUND.
IN ANY AND EVERY CIRCUMSTANCE,
I HAVE LEARNED THE SECRET OF FACING PLENTY AND HUNGER,
ABUNDANCE AND NEED.
I CAN DO ALL THINGS THROUGH HIM WHO STRENGTHENS ME.

God Expects us to Have Faith

In his article 'Life's not fair,' Travis Bradberry states that "Letting your doubts cloud your belief in someone (or something) practically ensures their failure. Medical professionals call this the "nocebo" effect." The Nocebo effect is the result of negative expectations in your life. We've talked a lot about expectations that are too high, but expectations that are too low are just as destructive.

Some couples come to us with a 'we'll make this work' kind of attitude. When we see that, we know that there is a good chance that the couple will indeed be able to work things out and come out the other side with a healthy marriage. Other couples come with a 'this will never work' attitude, and they're right. It won't work because negativity rather than faith surrounds their thinking.

If you are struggling with the 'nocebo' effect, then faith is the antidote. It comes through renewing your mind with the Word of God. Letting God give you the hope that is missing. Just to clarify the hope needs to be in God rather than in your spouse, after all, He is the one who is capable of turning your situation around.

Hebrews 11:1 (NIV)
Now faith is confidence in what we hope for and assurance about what we do not see.

When Expectations Go Very Wrong

Abuse in a relationship can be spiritual, emotional or physical. Unfortunately, sometimes people experience all three. God's purpose for marriage was companionship, help, love, support, fruitfulness and fulfilment. Control and any kind of abuse or manipulation are not part of God's design. There is no room for abuse in a Christ-centred marriage, yet, we see it to varying degrees in a lot of relationships. It can take many forms and a whole spectrum of severity. You may be surprised to find areas in your own marriage which are not healthy but abusive.

Usually, when we think of abuse in relationships, it's the horrendous cases that come to mind. But to be honest, we all are guilty of hurting our spouse to some degree. A little selfishness here or a little manipulation there and it can all add up to a relationship that is drawing away from serving God's purposes for us both and into something that serves our own purposes at the expense of our spouse's welfare.

Even a simple case of grumpiness, brought on because our spouse didn't give us the attention we wanted (sexual or otherwise) can be manipulative. Or if they didn't agree to an event or function you wanted to attend together, and your response is to give them the silent treatment, it's not behaving in a loving way towards each other. Watch out for the little things that divert your relationship from God's intentions for you that day.

Instead of a mutually beneficial relationship filled with a sense of wellbeing, the potential joy has vaporised leaving two adults emotionally crippled. I think we can all identify times in our marriages where we are guilty of running scenarios like this. I am certain all of us have been on both ends of manipulating or being manipulated. It happens when we focus on our own needs rather than those of our spouse.

We have to develop a culture within our marriages where we try to make each other's life easier. If we do this for each other, then we both benefit. We both have a great sense of welfare within our relationship, and we both reap the benefits of serving each other. Things go wrong when we try to get our own way.

Emotional Abuse

The following list of emotionally abusive behaviours is quite shocking and they go against every principle that that God gives us in 1 Corinthians 13:4-8 (NIV).

Love is patient, love is kind. It does not envy, it does not boast, it is not proud. It does not dishonor others, it is not self-seeking, it is not easily angered, it keeps no record of wrongs. Love does not delight in evil but rejoices with the truth. It always protects, always trusts, always hopes, always perseveres. Love never fails.

Can you recognise any of these in your relationship?

- Withholding
- Restricting
- Isolating
- Threatening
- Abandoning
- Raging
- Constant criticism
- Ridiculing
- Demeaning
- Coercing

- Accusing
- Ordering
- Ignoring
- Minimising
- Subtle nonverbal cues
- Denying one's reality
- Negative labeling
- Chronic deceit
- Belittling

It's quite a list! Although society has a tendency to dismiss emotional abuse it's important to recognise that it is very destructive in a marriage. It undermines the relationship by taking it on a downward spiral created by selfishness.

ABUSERS DO NOT CHANGE BY RECEIVING COMPASSION;
THEY CHANGE BY LEARNING TO GIVE IT.
EMOTIONAL ABUSE DOES NOT RESULT FROM STORMS OF ANGER;
IT EMERGES DURING DROUGHTS OF COMPASSION.
STEVEN STOSNY, PH.D.

This is a fascinating insight. Emotional abuse is symptomatic of a loveless relationship. If you are in the situation where you don't mind hurting your spouse with your words, attitude or actions then it's important to ask God to end the drought of compassion in your relationship.

Compassion is an attribute that Jesus showed again and again in His interactions with people but it should also be something that defines us as Christians. Colossians says we should clothe ourselves with compassion, it's something you actively need to do.

COLOSSIANS 3:12 (NIV)
THEREFORE, AS GOD'S CHOSEN PEOPLE,
HOLY AND DEARLY LOVED,
CLOTHE YOURSELVES WITH COMPASSION,
KINDNESS, HUMILITY, GENTLENESS AND PATIENCE.

Spiritual Abuse

Although we have said that you should study and apply the Scriptures, we want to throw in a warning. People have often taken scriptures out of context and misused them for their own gain. This is not the same as application; this is spiritual abuse!

Too many scriptures have been twisted and misunderstood over the years. Earlier we were careful to use the word study, not just read. That means finding out the context, making sure it fits with the other things that God says about marriage and relationships and understanding the original meaning.

Paul's leadership style wasn't authoritarian. In fact in 2 Corinthians we get to see his approach.

2 Corinthians 1:24 (NIV) Not that we lord it over your faith, but we work with you for your joy, because it is by faith you stand firm.

In a marriage, if one of you is spiritually lording it over the other then it should be a warning signal that something is out of balance. Paul sets the example to work alongside each other. Joy should be a fruit of the spiritual side of your relationship, it shouldn't be dread or fear because of spiritual intimidation or manipulation.

Some other signs of spiritual abuse in marriage include:

- Distorted view of respect

- Control-oriented leadership

- Quoting scriptures out of context

- Demanding submission and unquestioning loyalty and obedience

- A focus on spiritual performance rather than authenticity

- Using spiritual guilt

- Expecting grace but won't give grace

- Controlling through fear especially the fear of God

That's why God makes it really clear how we are to love each other. He puts a special emphasis on how men are to love their wives. Although spiritual abuse is not limited to being a male tendency.

Ephesians 5: 28-29 (NIV)

In this same way, husbands ought to love their wives as their own bodies. He who loves his wife loves himself. After all, no one ever hated their own body, but they feed and care for their body, just as Christ does the church.

Physical Abuse

Unfortunately, domestic abuse will affect 1 in 4 women and 1 in 6 men in their lifetime. That means that a certain percentage of those reading this book will have experienced violence in their relationship. We all have our own ideas of what constitutes physical abuse, but it's worthwhile using this opportunity to define it. A UK government document describes it like this.

- Hitting. Slapping. Pushing. Kicking.

- Misuse of medication. Restraint.

- Rape and sexual assault or sexual acts to which the adult has not consented, or could consent, or was pressured into consenting.

- Includes acts of omission.

- Ignoring physical or medical care needs.

- Failure to provide access to appropriate health, social care or educational services.

- Withholding necessities of life e.g. medications, nutrition, heating.

In other words, physical abuse is the absolute opposite of caring for your spouse's needs and protecting role that God has given. There are so many verses that tell us to care for one another, to be considerate of one another, to value one another.

Sometimes people get a bit offended at 1 Peter 3:7 because they read it as though the wife is weak. We like the way the Berean Study Bible puts it.

HUSBANDS, IN THE SAME WAY, TREAT YOUR WIVES WITH CONSIDERATION AS A DELICATE VESSEL, AND WITH HONOUR AS FELLOW HEIRS OF THE GRACIOUS GIFT OF LIFE, SO THAT YOUR PRAYERS WILL NOT BE HINDERED.

There is a difference in the female frame compared to the male frame. God expects husbands to be understanding toward their wives to love them and to cherish them. For you to cherish your wife requires that you recognise that they are something that is of great value.

PROVERBS 18:22 (ESV)
HE WHO FINDS A WIFE FINDS A GOOD THING
AND OBTAINS FAVOUR FROM THE LORD.

While other verses in Proverbs also emphasise the precious gift that God has given when you have been blessed with a spouse.

PROVERBS 31:10 (NIV)
A WIFE OF NOBLE CHARACTER WHO CAN FIND?
SHE IS WORTH FAR MORE THAN RUBIES.

Rubies are an incredibly rare and precious stone; I was surprised that they are even more valuable than most types of diamond. If you really appreciate and value your spouse, it is much less likely that you will mistreat them.

Ephesians takes the concept of love to a whole new level. The instructions are absolutely clear. There is no room for selfishness, neglect or abuse. God expects husbands and wives to care for each other in a self-sacrificing way.

Ephesians 5:28-30 (esv)

In the same way husbands should love their wives as their own bodies. He who loves his wife loves himself. For no one ever hated his own flesh, but nourishes and cherishes it, just as Christ does the church, because we are members of his body.

Philippians challenges Christians to change their focus from self to others. To change from pride to humility, to change from wanting what pleases us to what pleases others.

Philippians 2:3-4 (esv)

Do nothing from selfish ambition or conceit,
but in humility
count others more significant than yourselves.
Let each of you look not only to his own interests,
but also to the interests of others.

Why Abuse Happens

Selfishness

It's important to get some level of understanding why abuse happens. Marriage Builders suggests that "Abusive behaviour usually begins when a couple tries to resolve a conflict the wrong way. Instead of finding a solution that meets the conditions of the Policy of Joint Agreement (never do anything without an enthusiastic agreement between you and your spouse), an effort is made by one spouse to force a solution on the other. Resistance to the proposal is matched by increasing force until the spouse browbeats the other into submission. Every fight is an example of abuse because it uses the tactic of emotional or physical force to resolve a conflict instead of respect and thoughtfulness."

When you constantly push for your own way, it usually boils down to selfishness. Usually, before a couple gets married they do everything to please and attract the person they hope to marry. It comes as a shock to the system when selfishness kicks in. Unfortunately, some adults can behave like tantruming two-year-olds or manipulative teens in order to get what they want.

Many people find that the cost of winning an argument or getting their own way can be losing their relationship.

BLAME

Dr Steven Stosny attributes abusive behaviour to the root cause of blame. "Anger and abuse in relationships begin with blame: "I feel bad, and it's your fault." The person you blame also receives the brunt of your anger. It has been our observation that that blame occurs because of false expectations. It's especially true when you believed that the person you are married to would be the source of your happiness and remove the brokenness.

When you place high expectations on your spouse and expect them to meet those expectations, it is akin to idolatry, especially when that expectation is that they pander to your every need. You are placing your hope, your happiness and your future in the hands of someone who is human, and you are expecting them to behave like God. Just as the Israelites were guilty of setting up idols in their homes, it's possible to be guilty of setting up your spouse to be a 'false god'.

The problem is obvious; you begin to place your hope of happiness in a god which is false. A god which is flawed, a god who will ultimately fail, a god which we place blame upon and reject because they disappointed you. Yet, whose problem is it really? Doesn't it all boil down to your false expectations and idolatry?

The Bible is very clear about what should be done to false gods; they need to be torn down. That doesn't mean that you should reject your spouse and go out and find another false god who looks nicer, acts nicer and smells better. In a marriage, this means stop expecting your spouse to meet the needs that only God can meet. Go to the true God, who is trustworthy and faithful and is the only one who can meet your need.

Fundamental Attribution Error

Proverbs 13:12 (ESV)
Hope deferred makes the heart sick,
But desire fulfilled is a tree of life.

This is a symptom we, unfortunately, see in many marriages. Couples who have had high hopes but have become heartsick and disappointed. Many marriages are 'ill' or dying because of failed expectations and yet God's Word says that a desire which is fulfilled is a tree of life. A fresh start can be made; God can change your marriage from a hopeless one to one full of hope!

One hindrance though to a healthy future is if you are suffering from fundamental attribution error. It is an unhealthy distortion which affects who gets the credit and who gets the blame in your relationship. FAE is slightly different than basic blame, it points to an entirely warped perception of how your relationship works and prevents you from ever being able to appreciate your spouse.

While some disappointments certainly lie at your spouse's feet, not all do. If you have a tendency to blame everything on them, then you need to ask God to help you see things the way He sees things. When we fall into fundamental attribution error, then our spouse is usually the one who suffers most. They get all the blame when things go wrong but rarely get any credit when things go well.

Examples

Meals:

- If I cook a nice meal, it's because I am talented.

- If I burn the dinner, it's because my spouse was late.

Driving:

- If I get a speeding ticket, it's because the police needed to meet their quota.

- If my spouse gets a speeding ticket, it's because they were reckless.

Overspending:

- If I overspend, it's because everything has become so expensive and my spouse doesn't earn enough.

- If my spouse overspends it's because they can't handle money, they are irresponsible.

In other words, we explain any bad behaviour or underperformance on our part in terms of mitigating circumstances. There is no grace there for your spouse though, and you are more than happy to apportion blame and judge their character. When you assume responsibility for your actions and properly accredit and encourage your spouse in theirs, you will see your marriage transform.

FEAR

The list of things which summarises abusive behaviour all boil down to the desire to control. Abuse is when one person asserts control and authority over another's life through emotional, psychological, spiritual, physical or sexual manipulation. In all cases it is unacceptable!

That control is often the result of fear. Fear of what will happen, fear of failure, fear of isolation, fear that someone will find out that they are inadequate, fear of shame. There is a saying that hurt people hurt people. Control and abuse stem from deep identity issues. It is a sign of deep brokenness.

- Can you identify any of the following in your relationship?

  - Selfishness

  - Blame / Fundamental Attribution Error

  - Fear

What to Do if Abuse Happens

If You Are the Victim

If you are the subject of domestic abuse, then you have to do something about it. These situations don't just go away on their own. The abuse is negatively affecting your quality of life and places you in danger. It is even more important that you reach out for help. We would love to say that the church is able to help but that is not always the case, but the church should be the first place that you reach out to. This also means that the church should be prepared to help (by at least being aware of counsellors or organisations that those needing help can be referred to) when someone reaches out.

- Pray for the strength to ask for outside help.

  - Don't let shame or fear keep you in silence.

  - If you have been intimidated into keeping quiet about the abuse it is all the more important that you receive the help, support and protection that you need.

- If you are at risk of physical harm then it's important to find a safe place.

  - Some people struggle with a false sense of responsibility to dutifully remain in a dangerous situation.

- If your spouse is honest about needing help, they will be willing for you to be in a safe place until they are safe to be with.

1 Peter 5:7 (NIV)
Cast all your anxiety on him
because he cares for you.

Prayer and discernment are essential to break abuse patterns, you will need others to walk along side you on this journey.

If You are the Abuser

If you have found that you sometimes try to control your spouse's behaviour and attitude, then you need to ask God to show you the root cause. Is fear or something else at the heart of your conduct? You may need counselling to help you dig deeper and deal with the issues. Whatever you do though don't ignore the problem! We all need God to shine His light on us and ask Him to show us what we need to change.

Pray

- Prayer takes us from natural effort to supernatural power.
  - True and lasting change only comes through the power of prayer rather than willpower.

Repent

James 5:16 (ESV)

THEREFORE, CONFESS YOUR SINS TO ONE ANOTHER AND PRAY FOR ONE ANOTHER, THAT YOU MAY BE HEALED. THE PRAYER OF A RIGHTEOUS PERSON HAS GREAT POWER AS IT IS WORKING.

- Firstly confess your abuse to your spouse and seek forgiveness.

  - Recognise that this is not going to fix everything it's not a magic wand, but it is the first step.

  - Don't expect that your confession and seeking forgiveness will instantaneously repair your relationship. In the same way that saying sorry for dropping a plate doesn't fix the plate, your apology won't fix your spouse. They still suffer the emotional bruising you caused.

Get Help

- Confess your sin and ask for help and prayer.

- Agree to counselling - your abusive tendencies are rooted in areas where you are broken and need God's healing touch.

  - Not every church is equipped to deal with this problem effectively.

  - We would strongly recommend that this person should be a professional Christian counsellor who is used to working in this field.

STUDY

- One tool that God uses to change our mindsets is the Word of God.

- Don't just skim through or try to get through a lot of chapters. Ask God to speak to you through His Word and take the time to digest what He says.

APPLY

- If you are willing to read and apply the Bible to yourself (not only to others) you will start to see your thinking transform.

BE ACCOUNTABLE

- Surround yourself with people who know you well and love you well enough to tell you the things you may not want to hear.

THIS REMAINS TRUE:
BOTH THE ABUSED AND THE ABUSER NEED GOD TO INTERVENE
AND MAKE THEM WHOLE.

Releasing from Expectations

Asking for forgiveness and forgiving is a crucial element in any relationship. It is especially important in marriage. It is important that we ask forgiveness for the times when we fail or hurt our spouse.

One area of our relationships that also requires a forgiving attitude is in the area of expectations. We have already talked a lot about unrealistic expectations and disappointments and how they can damage our marriages. The way to deal with the effects of unrealistic expectations and disappointments is through forgiveness. It would be a healthy exercise now to examine the areas where you have been disappointed in your relationship because you hold unrealistic expectations about your spouse and their role within your marriage. We want you to prayerfully examine this. Allow the Holy Spirit to show you where your expectations have brought disharmony into your relationship. Ask Him when you need to confess this and ask for forgiveness.

Some things you can deal with immediately, others need time - prayer, possibly fasting to prepare the heart of your spouse for receiving your confession. You may need Pastoral support through this process. Their advice and prayer.

Expect to Blessed

It's easy to use a word like blessing without thinking much about what it really means. The word in Greek is Makarios (μακάριος). It means to be blessed, happy, fortunate and to be envied. That is what God wants for each one of you, that is what God wants for your marriage! When you put your trust and hope in the Lord, then you can expect His blessing.

This is not a performance based expectation. Those type of expectations cause incredible pressure, lead to disappointment, perpetuate failure and end in blame. God is the only one that is totally reliable. Even if life doesn't seem smooth blessing can still be our portion. In the sermon on the mount (Matthew 5:2-12), Jesus uses the word blessing again and again, but he pairs the word blessing with the things that we wouldn't necessarily count as blessings.

Blessed are the poor in spirit, ...
Blessed are those who mourn, ...
Blessed are the meek, ...
Blessed are ...those who hunger and thirst after righteousness, ...the merciful, ...the pure in heart, ... the peacemakers and the persecuted.

Why were all these people blessed? Because they had a promise. Each one had something to look forward to;

they had a reward, an inheritance. No matter what they were going through God was their reassurance that He would meet their need.

So many people live their married lives like they are under a curse. They behave as though they had been cursed with a life sentence. They struggle to see the blessing in it at all. We've already talked about the fall and how that impacted the relationship between Adam and Eve. When God designed marriage, He designed it to be a blessing. He didn't design it to be something we would hate or despise. He didn't design it to be something we would simply suffer through and come to the place where we considered it to be far from a gift in our lives.

Another translation of the word blessed, which is a slight variation of the word used here is: to be fully satisfied. Let's clarify this; it isn't just being satisfied when everything is going well, but it is satisfaction in spite of the circumstances. It's possible to have a blessed marriage; that is strong and that is fully satisfying in spite of what is going on around you.

Are there any areas of dissatisfaction that you need to take to God? Do you struggle to focus on the positive things instead of honing in on the negative? Perhaps you have journeyed through life and have continually asked yourself the question, 'Why God? Why did this happen to me?' Instead of asking the why question try asking the what question instead. 'What do you want me to learn from this situation Lord? What do you want to change in me?' As you change your focus you will find that your attitude starts to change.

FINALLY

It's obvious that you have a desire to see your marriage improve. You wouldn't have read this book if that was not the case. We want to encourage you that it isn't just a dream to have a blessed marriage. We have walked through nearly three decades together as a married couple, and we have discovered that we have needed to adjust a lot along the way. The biggest readjustment was in our attitudes and expectations. It's our prayer that this book has helped you adjust your expectations and that you will be blessed! It's also our prayer that you will be able to move forward together with a new love for each other and that you will give each other grace to change.

BIBLIOGRAPHY

Beliefnet's Inspirational Quotes
http://www.beliefnet.com/quotes/christian/hhenri-nou-wen/our-life-is-full-of-brokenness-broken-relationsh.aspx#6q6dJcimkrfQihym.99

Covenant Eyes Internet Accountability and Filtering. Covenant Eyes Pornography Statistics 250+ facts, quotes, and statistics about pornography use (2015 Edition) 2015-porn-stats-covenant-eyes.pdf
http://www.covenanteyes.com/pornstats/

Fight the New Drug. Why Porn Leaves You Lonely. Fightthe-newdrug.org August. 8, 2014
http://fightthenewdrug.org/why-porn-leaves-you-lonely/

Fileta, Debra.Men, STOP Looking for a Super Model Wife.
In Advice and Encouragement, For the Guys, Marriage, Single August. 9, 2016
http://truelovedates.com/men-stop-looking-for-a-super-model-wife/#sthash.GLm6wKMt.dpuf

Hertfordshire Government UK Information Base.
http://www.hertfordshire.gov.uk/infobase/docs/pdfstore/app2signs.pdf

Hitchman, Lainey. Life for Singles.Hitched Publishing. 2015

Kircher Jake & Melissa. Does Media Distort Love? A look at our corrupting views of romance, relationships and sexuality.

Relevant Magazine. April 12, 2011
http://www.relevantmagazine.com/life/relationship/
features/25275-distorting-love#D1zDB4xqOI7yLGKY.99

Lucado, Max. The Lucado Life Lessons Study Bible, eBook:
Inspirational Applications for Living Your Faith.
Thomas Nelson Inc, 2010 NKJV.

Rainey, Dennis & Barbara. Rekindling the Romance.
Thomas Nelson Publishers, 2007.

Science Daily
https://www.sciencedaily.com/terms/nocebo.htm

Stosny, Steven Ph.D. Anger in the Age of Entitlement. What
Drives Emotional Abuse and How to Begin to Recover. A look
inside lives spent walking on eggshells. June, 10. 2015
https://www.psychologytoday.com/blog/anger-in-the-age-
entitlement/201506/what-drives-emotional-abuse-and-
how-begin-recover

Thomas, Gary. How Porn Creates Angry Men. August. 10,
2016
http://www.garythomas.com/how-porn-creates-angry-men/
Torio. Miliquid moloribus es dolupitiunt landeliquia est aut
volecta tecupta quatiis inti idel int quid que consequ atem-
porentem exeribus, si sequi con nestruptate vent.
Adi officiiscidi offic to cuptassitem id quiate prorro omnis re
as et am quatia autem untiundae. Ariossinctis praestias

BIOGRAPHY

Roy and Lainey Hitchman met at university in the late 80's. Roy was studying aeronautical engineering and was on the university rowing team. Lainey was studying English and had a love of coffee. They got married during their student years, and God started to stir their hearts to help people navigate their relationships.

They have been ministering to families since 1993. Their passion for working with relationships led to them founding a ministry called 'Hitched' which encompasses working with a wide variety of relationships through a number of stages in life. Roy and Lainey share hard-hitting yet life-giving principles through transparency and humour.

Roy and Lainey spend much of their time speaking, writing and reaching out to those who need some encouragement in the area of relationships. When they aren't travelling, they enjoy spending time with their family, Ryan, Beth, Erin and their son-in-law Jonathan although it takes a little organisation to get everyone in one place at one time.

If you would like to learn more about their ministry, find more resources or get in touch you can contact them through www.hitchedtogether.com or www.lifeforsingles.com. If you would like them to speak at your church, seminar or conference, then please contact them via email at info@hitchedtogether.com

Lightning Source UK Ltd.
Milton Keynes UK
UKOW05f1003011216
288910UK00009B/275/P